PRAISE FOR P/
TH1

2009   One Book, One Columbus Selection
2007   Nebraska Book Award, sponsored by the Nebraska Center for the Book, fiction category
2007   Alex Award selection
2006   Holiday Barnes & Noble Discover Great New Writers selection

"Joern intricately weaves together a compelling family saga and a beautifully rendered paean to the land her characters love and are struggling to preserve. . . . Joern's lyrical and painterly descriptions of the vast Sandhills are the perfect backdrop for this subtle drama."
—*Booklist*

"Joern is particularly skilled at depicting contemporary small-town life and the issues rural communities face: the difficulty small farmers and ranchers have staying afloat financially and the decision of younger generations either to leave for urban areas or to endure directionless lives. She packs a lot of story into 250 pages."
—*Library Journal*

"Joern's characters are as stern as the land, and the world of her debut novel is sturdy and memorable."
—*Publishers Weekly*

"[Joern] is a fearless teller of hard truth. Set in the Sandhills of Nebraska, *The Floor of the Sky* is a tale of quiet heroics, a story of tenacity and courage, an intimate glimpse into the lives of independent ranchers determined to survive. A powerful portrayal of family, land, and loyalty. We are the wiser for having read it."
—**Sheila O'Connor**, author of *Where No Gods Came* and *Tokens of Grace*

"[Joern's] characters are sensible, endearing, and deeply haunted, and there's enough story and intrigue for ten novels. Secrets, old and new, keep the past constantly bumping into the present, making for a mesmerizing family saga."
—**Timothy Schaffert**, author of *The Singing and Dancing Daughters of God*

"Pamela Carter Joern writes with compassion and a wry sense of humor, in a direct and true style that takes in the vivid details of the world of the Nebraska Sandhills and the complexities and nuances of her characters' inner lives. Her work may bring to mind the novels of Kent Haruf and Larry McMurtry—though, like the fiercely independent women that populate her novel, Joern is clearly an original!"
—**Dan Chaon**, author of *You Remind Me of Me*

"A testimony to the power of family secrets and the enduring legacy of the land."

—**Mary Clearman Blew**, author of *Balsamroot: A Memoir*

"[An] emotionally rich first novel about an unwed pregnant teen spending the summer with her grandmother in the hardscrabble Nebraska Sandhills. . . . Her visit stirs up long-simmering tensions for Toby, Toby's bitter sister Gertie, and George, who has worked on the farm for more than fifty years. . . . [George's] unspoken love makes for irresistible reading. . . . Think Paul Newman with Joanne Woodward. . . . A resonant love story, whatever the age of the lovers."

—*Kirkus Reviews*

PRAISE FOR PAMELA CARTER JOERN'S NOVEL
TOBY'S LAST RESORT

"A lovely story, told with straightforward grace. Award-winning author Joern has won herself a new reader."

—**Micki Fuhrman**, *Roundup Magazine*

"This is a kindhearted, humorous, and graceful novel full of secrets, regrets, and redemptions. I immediately related to the drama of this beautifully drawn book about an eclectic cast of characters during a summer on the prairie and Sandhills of western Nebraska. Pamela Carter Joern writes about the Great Plains with the authority of a biologist and the passion of a poet."

—**Nickolas Butler**, author of *Shotgun Lovesongs* and *Godspeed*

"*Toby's Last Resort* is both lyrical and riveting. The writing is beautiful, the plot intricate, and the characters fully developed. The setting in the Nebraska Sandhills is inspired. Joern demonstrates with every page how the lives of ordinary people, when closely examined, are always extraordinarily complex, heartbreaking, and important. I loved every aspect of this fine novel and recommend it to all."

—**Mary Pipher**, author of *Women Rowing North*

"Pamela Carter Joern understands the flinty women of western Nebraska like few other writers. *Toby's Last Resort* is a beautiful, funny, and wrenching story that explores the love of land accompanied by a desire for independence and privacy. I loved this novel."

—**Maureen Millea Smith**, author of *When Charlotte Comes Home*

"There is a lovely solemnity to the lives of these characters—a hardness that Joern knows is alloyed with an abiding tenderness. That undercurrent is carried along in deceptively simple prose, writing that is stunningly clear."

—**Jane Hamilton**, author of *The Book of Ruth* and *A Map of the World*

"A moving family saga full of memorable characters whose struggles to survive the hardships of rural Nebraska life will haunt the reader."

—**Jonis Agee**, author of *The River Wife*

"Set against the backdrop of the Nebraska prairie, Joern's powerful second offering follows three generations as they navigate the greater part of the twentieth century. . . . Evocative prose elevates Joern's excellent portrayal of the family's evolution and brings a warmth and richness to a stark landscape."

—*Publishers Weekly*

"The clarity and honesty of Joern's prose impart a quiet intensity to this novel about three generations of a family enduring a hardscrabble existence in western Nebraska. Shaped by place and by each other, strong, flawed characters struggle through love and pain to create rich and dignified lives well worthy of our attention."

—**Tripp Ryder**, *Shelf Awareness*

"Joern has a gift for illuminating a character's inner life without speaking over much of it. She adeptly mixes past and present tense, effectively linking past and present, story and memory."

—**Pamela Miller**, *Minneapolis Star Tribune*

"As with [her] previous novel, *The Floor of the Sky*, Joern's writing is evocative and riveting, revealing her deep respect for those who live, and even thrive, on the plains."
—**Helene Williams**, *Historical Novels Review*

"With clean, polished and illuminating prose, Joern takes us through the highs and lows, marriage, divorce, children, disappointments, triumphs and sibling rivalries of several generations of one Nebraska clan. . . . It's a saga to be read again and again by an author who's already made a name for herself."

—**Barbara Rixstine**, *Lincoln Journal Star*

AT THE CORNER OF PAST AND FUTURE

A Collection of Life Stories

PAMELA CARTER JOERN

University of Nebraska Press | Lincoln

Acknowledgments for the use of copyrighted material appear on
pages 127–29, which constitute an extension of the copyright page.

The University of Nebraska Press is part of a land-grant institution
with campuses and programs on the past, present, and future
homelands of the Pawnee, Ponca, Otoe-Missouria, Omaha,
Dakota, Lakota, Kaw, Cheyenne, and Arapaho Peoples, as well as
those of the relocated Ho-Chunk, Sac and Fox, and Iowa Peoples.

For customers in the EU with safety/GPSR concerns, contact:
gpsr@mare-nostrum.co.uk
Mare Nostrum Group BV
Mauritskade 21D
1091 GC Amsterdam
The Netherlands

Library of Congress Cataloging-in-Publication Data
Names: Joern, Pamela Carter, 1948–author.
Title: At the corner of past and future: a collection
of life stories / Pamela Carter Joern.
Description: Lincoln: University of Nebraska Press, 2025.
Identifiers: LCCN 2024027750
ISBN 9781496242785 (paperback)
ISBN 9781496243140 (epub)
ISBN 9781496243157 (pdf)
Subjects: LCSH: Joern, Pamela Carter, 1948– | LCGFT:
Creative nonfiction. | Autobiographies. | Essays.
Classification: LCC PS3610.025 Z46 2025 |
DDC 814/.6 [B]—dc23/eng/20240905
LC record available at https://lccn.loc.gov/2024027750

Designed and set in Sabon Next by L. Welch.

For my brothers, Bob and Kent, who were there at my beginning.

In memory of Sally Hill and Don and Colleen Keyworth,
who guided my becoming.

Show him the sky.

—the response of an unnamed six-year-old to his science teacher when asked how to soothe a crying baby.

Posted by Nancy Bullard, Charlotte, North Carolina

Contents

Introduction

A life is made up of moments, intersections of time and place, memory and truth, life and art. Through all of it, we search for meaning. Patterns and purpose.

These pieces have been written over a long period of time. They touch on various aspects of my life: growing up in Nebraska, raising children, writing, surviving cancer. Some themes recur from different angles. If you know my fiction, you'll hear some echoes. When I set out to gather these writings into a manuscript, I thought I should have a definitive path. But life is messy. Things I planned for didn't happen; other things did. Most of the time, I feel either mildly lost or cheerfully sailing. Either way, I don't know where I'm going.

Over time, I've learned to think less about life as a destination.

Still, I am always seeking. I want to be awake in my life. I want my heart and spirit to twang with receptivity. These stories are my attempt to pay attention. I hope, at the very least, they show a mind at work.

AT THE
CORNER
OF PAST
AND
FUTURE

INTERSECTIONS of
TIME and PLACE

Looking for Direction

When I get homesick, it is for the landscape of Nebraska. I once said that to another self-exiled Nebraska native, and she had no clue what I was talking about. I don't know why land is more imprinted on one person than another. Perhaps it's as simple as preference, but I doubt it. It has more to do with circumstances of a childhood and whether you were driven to the land for recreation or for refuge. In my case, it was refuge. And it helped that I had a father whose soul was buried in the soil.

By the time I knew my father, he had given up farming. He sold the last of the machinery before I was born, when he was not yet forty. He had farmed in partnership with my grandfather, a man I never met, a man whose notorious stubbornness crystallized in his refusal to buy land. I've seen pictures of Gramp's bushy white hair, the lip cut away from cancer because he chewed tobacco, the glowing eyes. I try to imagine this fiery man in the same room with my gentle, poetic father. The story is that they adored one another, and perhaps they did, but when my father was thirty years old, married, living with his wife in a little house fifty yards from my grandparents' house, he was afraid to ask Gramp outright for the use of the pickup. Instead, he'd sit on the couch with his hat in his lap—my impatient mother swinging her legs at his side—and wait for Gramp to offer.

When Gramp died, Dad's ability to manage the land did not extend to dealing with landowners, bankers, or migrant workers. Plus, my parents had the bad luck of being hailed out several years in a row. Eventually, they held a farm sale. My mother, thirteen years younger than my father, claimed a new beginning. For Dad, the life he knew and loved was over. He worked various jobs for a while, suffered an emotional breakdown when I was eight, collapsed into early signs of illness. By the time I was sixteen, he was diagnosed with Parkinson's Disease. He died a week shy of my thirtieth birthday.

My dad wasn't much of a talker. Instead, I soaked him up through observation. He stood around outside, his hand on the head of our old hound dog, and watched the sky. He sat in a red upholstered chair and read a book on electronics or *Field & Stream*. One day he dragged home a castoff upright piano, and by nightfall he'd taught me to play "Twinkle, Twinkle Little Star" by ear. He retired to his workshop in the cellar and made things: a farm implement he later owned a patent on, a gadget for shelling corn, silky-sanded wooden toys for my brothers and me.

When I walk across the plains of western Nebraska, it is my dad who accompanies me. I put my feet down on the prairie grass and hope they will lead me to the lessons of the land.

WEST

My hometown is located in the heart of the North Platte River Valley in the western panhandle of Nebraska. The narrow valley consists of a few miles of prized farmland sandwiched between the Sandhills to the north and tableland to the south. The town itself, squat on the south bank of the river, stands at a crossroads of history, laced to the past by both the Oregon Trail and the Mormon Trail.

We lived seven miles west of town until I was ten years old. Riding to town once a week for groceries, I remember flat fields, wild roses along creek beds, single pinks and double yellows. Cattails and gold-enrod. There were two roads to town, both made of dirt and rutted. Washboard roads that made your voice shake if you tried to talk. Both passed over bridges that were occasionally washed out by heavy rain.

My parents, my two older brothers, and I lived in a tiny house. We called it the beet shack because it was originally built to house migrant workers on a neighboring farm.[1] I slept in a crib in the corner of my parents' bedroom until I was eight; then I was moved out onto the living room couch. If I squint my eyes, I can picture the inside of the house. I don't have to squint to see the outdoors. With one small step into the past, I taste the tang of well water, smell newly mown alfalfa, feel the grit of dust between my teeth, and hear the wind whine.

Outside, there was space. An extravagance of elbow room. We could see all the way to the horizon in the west, and when the sun set, pails of orange and pink and yellow and violet spilled over every corner of a vast dome. Stars crammed the sky at night. Clouds threw shadows over the ground, and we raced away from them, shrieking with laughter.

My brothers and I were allowed to roam free on the prairie. My parents trusted nature a lot more than they trusted people. We followed the lure of dragonflies up the road a quarter mile toward the schoolhouse. We crossed a cornfield to visit friends, stalks high above our heads rustling like crinkled tissue paper. We lived outside, seining dirt with an old window screen to lay down roads for our tractors and road graders. We made whistles of folded cottonwood leaves, blowing into them like a mouth harp. My brother would consent to play dolls only if we used my buggy for a covered wagon, and he drove it recklessly through ditches and across hazards of rotting boards. I trailed behind him, a peasant in his kingdom.

My brothers and I have big sky fever. I wonder if it is genetics that has done this to us. Are we the modern version of our stubborn grandfather, yearning for space, going west, refusing roots? Or are we merely suffering from the lifelong side effects of a hopeless love affair, chasing sky?

NORTH

After my father died, after my mother remarried, long after I had children of my own, I was desperate to go home in the autumn. School schedules had kept me from autumn in Nebraska for many years, and I wanted to see the fall grass swept with fire. I wanted to go alone, so in September I left my husband and children in Minneapolis and drove west.

"I want to visit all the places," I told my mother. "I want to make a map of your life. Let's drive out north of town."

Both my parents grew up on farms north of town. My dad lived on leased land; a half mile down the road was my mother's homeplace. Her parents were young with four small children, and they built the house with their own hands from a mail order kit. They planted orchards and grapevines. They had high hopes and, the way my mother told it, the yard was filled with laughter and love.

As happens too often, they didn't get what they wanted. My grandmother died of polio when my mother was eleven years old. The doctor called it paralysis of the throat, and she was sick less than a month. Her coffin was laid out in her parents' parlor in North Platte, where she was buried. My mother, her two sisters, and a brother were not allowed to touch their mother's body. Night after night, long after the funeral, my grandfather sat in the living room and cried, his four children huddled silently in the doorway.

Months later he hired the widow down the road to bake bread for his family. She was young, had two little boys, and had lost her husband in a farm accident. The widow, named Addie, had a younger brother who sometimes walked her down the road and helped with her parcels. When Addie married my grandfather, her brother technically became uncle to the stepchildren, but no one in the two families thought of themselves as related.

By the time my mother reached the age of seventeen and was set to graduate from high school, she had two new sisters, one of her stepbrothers had drowned, and her father had died in a haying accident.[2] Addie's brother, who was thirty, proposed marriage to my mother. Addie opposed the marriage but not strongly.

My parents were married in my mother's house. My mother got up early to milk the cows, wash the separator, and scrub the kitchen floor before the wedding took place at 10:00 in the morning. Her dress, ordered from the JCPenney catalogue, featured cream-colored cotton lace with blue piping and a blue-ribbon sash. It cost seven dollars.

Not long after my parents' wedding, Addie sold the farm. The house, the land, the vineyards, and the orchards slipped out of the family into other hands. When we drive north of town, it is only remnants that we see. My mother recites where everything originally stood, her voice heavy with sorrow.

One half mile away are the now deserted buildings where my father lived. On that autumn day of our expedition, Mom and I got out and walked around. The house stood far back from the road, hidden by a grove of trees. No doors, no windows, spiderwebs, dust everywhere. Nothing inside. It had been vacant for a long time.

North of town seems like a graveyard to me. Carcasses of houses. Memories of times gone by. Haunting thoughts of "might have been." Windbreaks are choked with dying elm trees. Loss and grief are hand-maidens out there on that lonesome piece of ground.

But there is something else, too. A wild rosebush clings to the bank of an irrigation ditch. A withered cedar offers shade. Sunflowers line the roadside. This may not be what you have in mind, the land says to me, but this, too, is life.

SOUTH

We moved to the south edge of town when I was ten years old. Farther south stood Courthouse and Jail Rocks, sandstone monuments that jut up out of the prairie as unexpectedly as an iceberg in the northern seas. Signs warn tourists not to attempt to climb the rocks and to watch for rattlesnakes. Courthouse, big and rectangular, is stacked in a series of diminishing plateaus like layers of a cake. It looks, from a distance, like an overgrown submarine. Jail Rock is narrower and shaped like an upside-down funnel. Between the two rocks are ravines that lead to Pumpkin Creek. The land around the monuments is dotted with sage and yuccas, milkweed and sunflowers.

By the time I was twelve, the Rocks were a favorite place. Once, a friend and I drove out with my mother as the sky was clouding up to rain. We wanted to climb, but my mother thought it was too dangerous since there might be lightning. We begged, charged with the invincibility of youth. We assured her that we could go to the top and back down in ten minutes, and against her protests we scrambled up, up, and then down in eight minutes flat. In later years I climbed with my husband and our two daughters, chiding them not to get too close to the edge. A cross near the top commemorated the death of a young man who fell while partying with friends.

Still years after that, my mother and I drifted out to the Rocks on a gray Sunday in March. We were soaked in grief, aimless in the way of recent mourners. My stepfather had died of a heart attack one month before. His ten-year marriage to my mother had been a resurrection experience for both, an unexpected reprieve after each had dealt with spouses with long-term illnesses.

Mom and I had spent the week taking care of affairs, and we were wrung out. We drove to the Rocks at dusk, when quiet drapes the day, and we walked the ravines. As we came up out of the canyons to return to our car, we heard a meadowlark. If the sky is golden and life is fair, the lilting song of the western meadowlark can make you think of carousels and wind chimes. But on a gray drowning day of grief, it's a mournful sound, a melancholy flute. A modest prairie bird, heavy-bottomed with a mustard-colored breast, nothing in the meadowlark's visage portends the beauty of its haunting song. We looked for the maker of the melody atop the nearby fence posts, but we could not see it.

My mother swore that the meadowlark sings *John Greenleaf Whittier*, the right number of syllables, even if it doesn't give you a clue as to the pitch of each note. *John Greenleaf Whittier, John Greenleaf Whittier*, Mom called, lifting her voice to join the song of a bird she had known all her life. Feeling foolish, I joined her. *John Greenleaf Whittier*. Not for a moment did I think the bird was fooled, but perhaps we were.

EAST

When I go home from Minneapolis, I often come in from the east. I turn off I-80 onto Highway 26 at Ogallala, where the landscape abruptly changes. This is where the west begins. Sage and yuccas replace cornfields. I used to bribe my children: fifty cents to the first to hear a meadowlark. The road winds around Lake McConaughy, past Ash Hollow and Windlass Hill, through a series of little towns: Lewellen, Oshkosh, Lisco, Broadwater. I am a buffalo chasing the scent of water. I am coming home.

Some years ago, my mother told me that of us three children, I had moved the furthest away from my upbringing. My oldest brother lived in California, so I knew she wasn't talking about miles.

"Mom," I said. "What do you mean? I have a husband and two kids. We are buying a three-bedroom house. We go to church every Sunday. I live a very conventional life."

"Yes," she said slowly. "But it's your thinking."

She's right, of course. Nebraska is the skeleton of my life, but it has been overlaid with other experiences that sometimes seem to obliterate the past. I walk the prairies, placing my feet in the footsteps of my land-loving father, but it is myself that I am searching for.

If I am home in the spring, I see flutters of white moths around clumps of yucca. I know that the plants and the moths are mutually dependent on one another. They exist in a symbiotic relationship. The flower of the yucca is constructed so that it cannot self-pollinate. The female moth pollinates the flower in the process of laying her eggs deep in the ovaries. The hatched larva feeds on the developed seeds, eventually bores a hole, and drops by a silken thread to burrow underground and wait for the following spring. Then it emerges as a full-grown moth, and the process starts all over again.

Sometimes I feel that I am that moth. I cannot get too far away from my roots, or I will forget who I am. I come back home, enter the familiar landscape, feed off the sky and grass, and disappear until the following spring.

I think about another relationship of the prairie. On the mesas of the high plains, underneath every dropped cow pie is a colony of termites. The termites could not exist without the moist and dark environment provided by dung. There is little wood lying around on the high plains, but there is plenty of dung and probably has been for more years than we care to count. Before cattle, there were buffalo, and before buffalo, there were mastodons. The termite and the minute protozoa that live inside the termite intestine need cellulose for continued life, and cellulose is present in wood or in dung. The relationship between termite and protozoa is, in fact, a mutual and symbiotic one. Neither could exist without the other. The relationship between the steer and the termite is another matter. To the termite, the existence of warm dung is a matter of life and death. The steer, however, has no awareness of the termite. To the steer, where he drops his waste is merely a matter of convenience.

It makes me uneasy, but I think my relationship to the land is much like that of the termite and the steer. I locate myself in that Nebraska landscape. I need it as surely as a body needs a skeleton, but the landscape is indifferent to my presence.

I took my daughters to western Nebraska every summer of their young lives. They walked the canyons with an eye out for snakes, clipped sage from the high plains, recognized the song of the meadowlark. I told them family stories, and I walked with them over the prairie. I found I could not teach them about the things I love. Some lessons can only be learned by observation, by putting your ear to the ground and listening to what the land has to say.

Forest and Prairie

When I stepped into the redwood forest near Santa Cruz, California, the first thing I noticed is that I could not see the sky. I craned my neck to follow the upward stretch of trunks as straight and bare as shafts of arrows for one hundred, two or even three hundred feet. Between the dense undergrowth and the lacy canopy of the treetops, a vast enclosed space. No wonder early pilgrims to this area spoke of cathedrals, steeples, and spires. It felt as though I had entered a world apart, and I dropped my voice instinctively to a whisper.

Forests have always seemed foreign to me, having grown up on the plains of western Nebraska. There you see an occasional cottonwood hunkered beside the remnants of a Sandhills spring or crowded by a farmer-planted windbreak of Siberian elms. Low lying Russian olive trees meander along the riverbanks and creeks. On the prairie, the eye is not drawn up as it is in the natural cathedrals of the redwood forest. Instead, the eye is drawn out, toward the horizon. From the top of Courthouse Rock, a sandstone monument south of my hometown, you can see faint Oregon Trail ruts stretching toward Chimney Rock fifteen miles to the west, the spine of the Wildcat Hills curving round toward Mitchell Pass, high arching sandhills some twenty-five miles to the north, and far below, at the base of the rock, like green frosted trim, a few trees following the curves of Pumpkin Creek. The land has texture, rising and falling as it drifts toward the horizon, dark and light as cloud shadows play across its surface. Over it all stretches an endless dome of sky. Space and sky and wings flow in a Nebraskan's blood, so that when I am in a forest, I hear my father's voice lamenting that hemmed-in feeling. I wonder if there will be enough air to breathe.

The air in the Henry Cowell Redwoods State Park on that February day seemed uncommonly still. It smelled moist and vaguely salty from the sea, not of pine like forests I have known but of earthy humus. The quiet was so dense, I felt I could put my hand out and stroke it. It had been a windy day along the coast when my husband and I drove up from Monterey, but under the awning of giant trees, the wind disappeared. We were well into the forest before we heard a gush of moving air, a whirring high in the treetops. The tall spires swished and swayed. Later, perhaps as much as five minutes, we still heard the tinkle of falling needles and tiny cones that the wind knocked loose. I stood still on the path for several moments hearing tiny tintinnabulations, delicate tracings of crick and crack, but little fell on me. The wind was a phantom. We saw the sway, heard the rush, tracked the ting of falling debris, but we never felt the wind touch us with its fingers.

On the plains, wind comes at you full in the face. It pulls at your hair, creases your clothing into the crevices of your body, suggests you go some way other than the one you planned. It roars across empty spaces, sweeping tumbleweeds into barbed wire fences, raising whirlwinds of unprotected field dust. As kids, we turned our backs to it, held out the bottoms of our shirts to create sails and let them carry us across the meadow.

As I stood in the redwood forest, I thought about wind and how, as a child on the plains, I learned there's not much use resisting it. You can't hide from it either. It howls around the corners of houses and seeps in through doorways and cracks, leaving fine filtered dirt behind. I wonder if that is how memory functions, howling around our crafted identities, seeping in through cracks in the facade, reminding us of who we are and where we've been. I brought Nebraska with me to this redwood forest; sky and wind are carved on the palms of my hands.

I also took Nebraska with me when I was transplanted to Minnesota forty years ago. We had only two days to purchase a house, having flown into Minneapolis for a weekend in February. I wanted a home with light and a feeling of space. We settled on a three-bedroom brick colonial across the street from a city park. The front yard was wide open because the elms on the city easement had died. Barren soccer fields covered the park that faced the house. From the front door, I would be able to see almost half a mile, my view extended across the front yard and through the park.

There was, however, one problem. There were two large overgrown yews smack against the east windows on the front of the house, one on either side. They were depressingly healthy and at least ten feet tall. They not only blocked the view, but they shrouded the living room and dining room in darkness. From the day we bought the house in February until the Fourth of July weekend that we moved in, I lobbied for the removal of those trees.

We didn't know our neighbors well enough to consult or even consider their views. On the day when the trees were removed, several people wandered by. Our immediate neighbor to the south stood in the front yard and watched the efforts of the workmen. "Those sure are pretty trees," he said to me. The neighbor to the north, an older man whose lot was crowded with maples, firs, and birches, merely said, "We love trees."

I recited Joyce Kilmer's "Trees" as a child. I spent hours draped in the arms of a cottonwood. But I realized, as I walked around neighborhoods in Minneapolis, something else was going on here. Many yards held overgrown, sparse, half-dead evergreens that I would not have tolerated. Windows were draped by shadow and, in many cases, blocked by trees. Ads in newspapers bragged about wooded lots I saw one house where a tree had been allowed to shove its way through the roof of the porch.

The difference between me and my neighbors, when it comes to trees, has much to do with my love of space and their love of shelter. Where they talk about cozy, I feel claustrophobic. A friend of mine who grew up nestled in Minnesota forests says that when she is on the prairie, she feels untethered, as if she could fly off into space. I nod and say, I know; I love that feeling. Nostalgia also plays a part in determining our preferences. My Minnesota friends recall childhoods spent among the pines; I conjure up hayfields and chokecherry hollows. Trees speak to Minnesotans of permanence, history; space speaks to me of possibility.

Inside the redwood forest, I stood within the shadows, longing for sky, but I was undeniably moved by the beauty of the stately trees. They were impressive, and not only because of their size.

As a hardy Nebraskan, I was struck by the resilience of the coastal redwoods. They have developed an arsenal to deal with a wide range of assaults. The thick bark protects the heartwood of the tree from fire. We saw trunks with hollowed out fire scars, domed spaces lacquered in flat black, large enough for me to stand in. Other trees had been more seriously damaged, but new growth sprouted from each blackened stump in what is called a *fire column* because it follows the route laid out by the flames. Some trees die on top but are green below. We came upon one of these *spike-tops*, but the foliage was so high above my head that I could not see the top of the tree. One rotting stump, having succumbed at last, was the home of several new plants, among them a young redwood and a mountain laurel.

Besides resistance to fire, the redwood is impermeable to floods. Because of its great height, it is not smothered by rising soil levels. It simply generates a vertical root through newly deposited soil and creates a lateral root system at the new level. One tree survived seven floods, nine fires, the loss of over half its trunk surface, and damage to its root supply. It maintained itself, a bulk estimated at a million pounds, for 113 years in that condition until it finally fell in 1933. It was measured to be 310 feet tall, taller than a football field is long, higher than a thirty-story skyscraper.

In addition to its defenses for existing trees, the coastal redwood has adapted to several methods of regeneration. The most common method is sprouting from the roots, which results in a grouping of trees, like organ pipes. We saw one huddle of seven trees around the lip of a crater, where the mother tree had died. They gathered like druids in a ceremonial circle, their tops swaying over them in cloaks of secrecy.

Two of the druid group of trees wore large warty growths called burls that looked like lumpy knapsacks of mythical gnomes. Inside each burl are hundreds of buds. If placed in water, they sprout like the eyes of a potato.

Finally, if all else fails, the redwood produces cones with seeds. The cones are ridiculously small. Each cone holds fifty to sixty seeds, and the seeds are so tiny that 123,000 might weigh a pound. As I stood and held a cone in the palm of my hand, I could not help but think this is a mighty joke. Yet, there is method to this folly. Although tiny, seeds are produced in staggering numbers, five million in one year from a single tree. The seeds lie dormant but fertile for as many as fifteen years. They rarely flourish in the dense undergrowth and poor light of a healthy redwood forest, but if a fire ravages the forest, then while the ground is bare and sterilized, the seeds stir into action.

By the time I had learned this much about the redwoods, I was beginning to feel as though these trees had intelligence, like the talking woods of Shakespeare. Not far ahead, in a bend of the path, I saw a redwood with a large branch thrust out at a right angle and then straight up, like an arm signaling a right-hand turn. Most redwood trunks are militantly straight, making them prized for lumber and reminding me of admonitions from childhood to stand tall. This second trunk was the tree's way of correcting a lean, something like a flying buttress. I marveled at such an invention and wondered how it signals itself to perform this clever mutation.

My starting point will always be the landscape of Nebraska. All other places are a matter of comparison, in the same way that my Minnesota friends measure the prairie against lakes and forests. I think these tensions are good for us. We have different imprints from the land that shaped us and crowds our memories. I can't say I'm sorry that we removed those yews from in front of our windows, but I am grateful that somebody had the good judgment to save the redwoods.

When I emerged from the redwood forest, I stepped into a bath of sunlight and open sky. I felt exactly the way I did as a kid when we walked out of my frail grandmother's house, free at last to run and talk out loud. I was glad to have made the visit, but it was time to go home. Shelter to vulnerability. Housed to freedom. Forest to prairie.

At the Corner of Past and Future

It is 1996, and the distance between my hometown and me is 800 miles and thirty years. Driving west across Iowa and Nebraska, I pass mile after mile of cultivated fields fit neatly together like a checkerboard. All these tidy plots make me think of hospital corners on once unruly beds. At Ogallala, I turn onto a two-lane highway. Obedient rows of corn give way to random sage and yuccas. The North Platte River twists and snakes. This is where the past begins, at this intersection of I-80 and Highway 26.

I am coming home for my thirtieth high school class reunion, and with me is my eighteen-year-old daughter. We've made this trip every summer of her life, sometimes with her dad and older sister. This year it is the two of us, and my daughter is worried about how she will occupy her time.

"What do you and Grandma do all day?" she asks me.

"Mostly talk. Run errands. It will work out."

I look at her out of the corner of my eye. She's long and lean with a boyish figure. Her blond hair is raked back into a knot at the back of her head. She has lovely hands but bites her fingernails, as she is doing now because she's bored. If I am moving toward the past, she is all future. I can feel it in the way she drums her fingers on the dashboard.

I didn't insist that she make this trip, but I'm glad to have her with me. She's been away for her first year of college, and I've missed her. Although we've never talked about it, I know my daughter has big sky fever. She is, like me, in love with the prairie. She is lured by windmills and lone cottonwood trees. She moves around the base of Courthouse and Jail Rocks as if in a house of prayer.

It's a long drive to western Nebraska from Minneapolis, two seven-hour days, and most of the time my daughter plugs into music or sleeps. I spend the time thinking about the past. I have not seen most of my classmates since our twentieth reunion. I grew up with a boy I'll call Tom and his younger brother. Let's call the brother Norm. We all went to a one-room country school together, along with ten other kids, two of whom were my big brothers. Except for one older girl and me, the rest were boys. Later, when we entered high school, Tom and I landed in different circles. Tom and Norm hovered on the fringe of trouble. In the parking lot of the Legion Hall, I once witnessed the two of them fighting, drunkenly ploughing each other with their fists.

Tom went on to college, married, became a coach and high school history teacher. Norm went to Vietnam and died on an unnamed battlefield. I remember Norm as a big, clumsy kid who cried easily. He talked tough, but it was all bluster. Too often, our teacher took him out in the school vestibule and whacked him with an oak paddle. Norm's face turned red with anger, and in his rage, he cried.

Years ago, I visited the Vietnam War Memorial in Washington DC. I located Norm's name on the shadowed wall, and I wept for that misunderstood kid who kept getting yanked out to the vestibule. I made a rubbing of his name on my pink airline itinerary, the only paper I had with me.

At our twentieth reunion, Tom and I stood talking. Tom wore blue jeans, cowboy boots, a white shirt with pearl snap buttons. He looked like Burt Reynolds playing a cowboy, except Tom was the real deal. I told Tom that I had a rubbing of Norm's name, and I offered to send it to him. He said he'd like to have it. He hoped to get to the memorial himself someday. After I got back home, I stuck the pink paper in the mail. Weeks later, I received a thank you from Tom's wife, a woman I don't know. She wrote that Tom had sent the rubbing on to their son, a first-year student at the Air Force Academy, and he had pinned it to his bulletin board.

Two years after that, I attended a fiftieth wedding anniversary in my hometown. My brother tapped me on the shoulder. "Got a surprise for you," he said. I followed him outside, and there stood my western hero, decked out in full regalia, including a tall white hat. We didn't say a word. I walked into Tom's hug, put my head back, and laughed up into his ruddy face.

It's been eight years since I've seen Tom. Driving across Nebraska, I wish that I'd had the chance to know a few more of my classmates as the people they have become. Most of them are stuck in my head at age seventeen. Chilled, I realize that I am stuck in the same place in theirs. I risk a glance in the rearview mirror. Older, wrinkles, and too many gray hairs. At my twentieth reunion, I was one of two women labeled the least changed. They meant outwardly, of course. No one knew of any changes in me that are deeper than my skin.

As my daughter and I drag down Main Street on the way to my mother's house, the thermometer on the bank registers 103 degrees. Heat hangs in the air and shimmers. It bends our vision like a mirage.

Main Street of my hometown is not what it used to be. Stores are boarded up or have been converted to small gift shops that offer country kitsch or a few bona fide antiques. You'd need a map to find your way back to this street's history. Where that insurance office sits, there used to be a movie theatre, a big old barn with loges in the back we had to pay an extra dime to sit in. Mr. Schmidt, the owner of the Trail Theatre, walked through from time to time to make sure all the teenagers were sitting up. Feet on the floor, he'd bark. Renner's Jewelry has been gone for years. Next to the old bank, in that empty lot, there was a public women's restroom. I used to thread my way through a narrow lounge where old women sat and crocheted. On the sidewalk out front, old men tipped their chairs back against the building and loaded their pipes with pungent tobacco. Carl's is going strong, and I wonder if Carl still prohibits women from his bar. When I was a teenager, my brothers and most other boys of the town hung out at Carl's in a heady atmosphere of smoke, male camaraderie, and the slap of pool shots. I look down the west side of the street. A sign over Bert's Five-n-Ten announces: Closing Out Sale.

We pull into the drive beside Mom's garden, crammed with tomatoes, peppers, and Swiss chard. Some years my mother swears the plants get smaller as the summer progresses, but she never gives up. She's waiting for us. I smell meat in the Crock-Pot. There's a freshly baked pie on the kitchen counter. I hope this time she remembered I don't like apple pie. Her voice rises several notes in pitch as she hugs us: How was the drive? Do you want anything? How about some iced tea?

My mother and I enjoy each other's company for about five days. That's not bad, and my daughter and I don't plan to stay any longer than that.

That evening, to get out of the house, the three of us take a walk around the Pits, a state recreation area west of town. The lakes here were originally sandpits. The water lies in holes like mirrors dropped down from helicopters. The banks are lined with gray Russian olive trees and glimmering cottonwoods. As we are driving away, we run into one of my classmates, astride a big Harley and shirtless, full black beard and still-black hair. We chat, mostly about the Sturgis biker festival, which he and his wife attend every year. On the way home, my mother says, "He has the nicest wife in town."

When I was ten, we moved to town against my father's wishes. He hated to be hedged in, but there was no other place to rent. On my first day of town school, I stood in a lavender plaid dress at the bottom of a giant flight of stairs leading up to the main lobby of the grade school. I chewed on my bottom lip. From out of nowhere, that same black-haired boy appeared. I knew him from Sunday School. "You're in my class," he said, motioning for me to follow him. He took the steps two at a time. I left my mother, and I was launched.

That boy and I were not close in high school. He was smart, good-looking, groomed to become part of his father's implement business, carefree (it seemed to me) in a way I couldn't afford. I was smart, churchy, careful, and, I felt, boring to a boy like him. A boy like him. What in the world did I imagine that to be? I didn't know him.

I know even less about the man he has become. But my mother says he has the nicest wife in town.

After two days of holing up inside because of the heat, my daughter comes to me quietly in the bedroom.

"Mom," she says. "We have to do something today. I have to get out of the house."

"Okay. Name it."

"I wouldn't mind if I could read," she whispers to me. "But you can't read around Grandma. She won't let you."

I smile at my daughter and the gift of understanding she doesn't know she's handed me. I have been a reader all my life, an irritation to my mother. Reading was my chief act of rebellion, carrying me to places where my mother couldn't follow. Once, after playing several rounds of cards, I pled for time to read. "Just a half hour," I said. This was years after I'd left home, when my visits were infrequent, and I understood my mother's desperation to squeeze every drop of togetherness. "All right," my mother said. She followed me into the next room. I propped a book in front of my face, and she went on talking.

These days when I look at my daughter, I see her on the brink of flight. She's taking off for regions where I don't belong. I work hard to resist trailing her from room to room.

My mother, my daughter, and I decide to make a trek out to Courthouse and Jail Rocks, sandstone monuments south of town that jut up out of the prairie like jagged teeth. I've climbed them often despite warnings posted about rattlesnakes. Today it's too hot to climb, so the three of us settle for tramping around by the creek. We swing out over the dry creek bed on ropes left by campers. I lift my mother to help her put her foot in the noose; she's not about to miss out on the swinging.

My daughter wanders off in a nearby field to take photographs with her 35mm camera.

"Be careful," I say.

"I know, I know. Snakes," she tosses back over her shoulder.

This place is used as a shooting range by a local rifle club part of the year. Mom and I climb up on the gun platforms and sit. She talks to me about all the family excursions made here. I listen with one ear, but mostly I cherish the sight of her. The thought of her, even. She's wearing a wide-legged pair of shorts, feet pulled up, her arms locked around her legs. She throws her head back and laughs.

I remember one summer when a baby eaglet was stranded out here. It had fallen from a high nest on the west wall of Jail Rock. It hadn't died in the fall, but it was trapped among the rocks at the base of the monument. We called the local authorities, who said its only chance for survival was for us to leave it alone. Only the mother could save it.

"We have to leave it be," Mom said. "But it doesn't have a chance."

We'd drive out each day to check on it. The mother eagle soared high overhead, mute and rag-winged, but she could do nothing to help her baby.

I think about this now as I watch my daughter move heedlessly through knee-high grass. I think about my mother, insisting that all of us go away to college, prepare ourselves for a life that would distance us from her. I know that if I had wings, I would tear them to pieces to save my child. I would give up my freedom for her, as my mother did, but it still would not keep distance from falling between us like a weighted curtain.

On the night of the reunion, I model both dresses that I've brought along. Mom votes for the short blue one. She says it makes me look young. My daughter says definitely the long brown one. Though suspicious of her motives—no eighteen-year-old thinks their mother looks young or needs to—I go with her instincts. My hair behaves like shredded wheat. The hot wind has dried it to a tumbleweed.

When I get to the reunion, I am met with the usual round of greetings and laughter. Thirty-nine of us have shown up out of a class of fifty. My best friend from high school lives in Florida and never comes home for these reunions. I am stunned overall at how old we look. Someone had the good sense to make lapel buttons out of our graduation pictures so we can identify each other. One of my classmates refuses to wear her button. She looks terrific, in great shape and prettier than she was as a teen.

I scan the room for Tom, but it turns out he has been waiting behind me. He takes me by the arm and pulls me to one side. He's been drinking and stands too close. His eyes are rheumy. He sways on his feet.

"I want to thank you for sending me that rubbing of Norm's name," he says, his speech slurred.

"It's okay," I say, pushing him gently on the shoulder. I want him to back off.

The night does not go well. I sit with my first crush and his beautiful wife, but they talk mostly with the couple they've stayed close to over the years. I learn that Tom is going through a tough time, in trouble for roughing up a student, a divorce, drinking. I'm saddened by this beyond all reason.

After dinner, the deejay starts up in the adjoining room. Another classmate is here without his wife, so he immediately asks me to dance. "You do dance?" he asks. The truth is I haven't danced a total of thirty minutes in my whole married life, but I figure I can fake it. I loved to dance in high school, and how hard can it be? It turns out to be a lot harder than I thought. My partner is now a dance teacher. He knows all the moves, and although he shows me one complicated pattern three times in a row, I can't get it right. We laugh a lot, but I am humiliated beyond repair. What happened to that girl I used to be? Feeling like a teenaged wallflower, I decide to leave early.

The next morning, as my daughter and I are heading out, Mom wants to know if I had a good time. I lie to her. Sure, I say. I am too raw to try to explain it. I don't understand it myself. For the first hundred miles I sort it over in my mind. What went wrong? Why couldn't I enjoy myself? What was I expecting that didn't happen? Why couldn't I get over my adolescent self? We are a mystery, even to ourselves, our lives opening to us like trapdoors sprung by a simple shift of weight.

I start to relax as we approach Ogallala. The road is my meditation, and distance grants me a different perspective. No matter how much I chase myself when I go home, I can't locate myself there. Life's intersections happen at a fixed point in time, the way these highways merge at a fixed point in space. I can't re-enter the past, any more than I can accompany my daughter into her future.

My daughter and I stop in Ogallala to load up on gas. I go inside to pay the bill, and when I emerge, she's in the driver's seat. The car is a Jeep, so she sits up high like a trucker. She leans her elbow out the window. She's wearing her John Lennon shades and dangling a candy cigarette from her lower lip. She looks down at me as I get closer to the car.

"C'mon, Ma," she says with a grin and a fake western drawl. "Let's blow this pop stand."

I climb into the shotgun seat. I flip on my old green sunglasses, stick a candy cigarette in my mouth. We tuck our love of this land into the bottoms of our knapsacks, and we head for home.

Standing in Lines

Once I became a stranger to myself and stood in line for two days to buy tickets to a Neil Diamond concert. An ill wind came over me, a possession of sorts, time collapsed, and years later, I struggle to tell my children why their mother once went berserk.

I had gone shopping with my four-year-old daughter. Behind towels and sheets on the third floor of a department store, we discovered a line of people, wrapped around a few counters and down an aisle. Needing to cross through the line, I made excuses and asked, What are you waiting for? Tickets, some said. Tickets to the Neil Diamond concert.

I casually stepped to the end of the line. It didn't seem like a big commitment. I had with me a book or two, a blanket, and a stuffed toy, and my daughter settled in. At noon, I asked someone if they'd hold my place in line while I bought us sandwiches and soda.

By 2:00, when the line hadn't progressed much, the young woman in front of us started to play Scissors, Paper, Rock with my daughter. I'd met Carl and Monica and Sylvia and Jerry, the people immediately surrounding us. We'd swapped tales of other concerts, chatted about what we did for a living, and wondered why it was taking so long.

At 4:00 my daughter and I had to leave because her sister was due home from school. I had to pry myself away. Like a gambler at the track, I hated to leave after investing so much.

That evening we heard the radio announce that, due to the demand for tickets, a second show would be added. The next morning, I dropped my daughter off at a mothers-day-out program and headed back to the scene of my seduction. In line, but closer to the front, stood Carl and Monica, Sylvia and Jerry. They let me slip in place with them, and we congratulated ourselves on our good fortune.

By noon it was clear the line was stalled. Computer problems, someone said. My friends held my spot, and I drove to pick up my daughter. Shameless, I had called ahead and asked a friend if she could spend the afternoon.

I stood in line again until 4:00. The last fifteen minutes were agony, inching closer to the window. When it became clear that I wouldn't make it, Sylvia said if she got to the window, she'd buy tickets for me. We exchanged phone numbers. We clasped hands. Parting was hard work.

Later that evening, Sylvia called and told me she had purchased two tickets for me. She offered to drop them off. I prepared the check. When she stood at my door, we suddenly realized that we were, after all, strangers. Shyness took over, and no amount of prodding would induce her to step inside. We handed off the tickets and the check, and I never saw her again.

When I look back at those two days, I am awed at the human capacity for numbness. I've taken long car trips when my mind and body entered a twilight zone. I've put myself on hold for hours in waiting rooms. I've been stuck in motels in bad weather. But why would anyone choose to put themselves through this?

I stayed because each moment that I invested upped the ante. I stayed because each next moment might be the winning one, the same reason people buy lottery tickets. I stayed because I got sucked in, and once in, it was difficult to get out. Like a movie about a crime that topples from innocence to multiple murders, one moment led to the next, and I couldn't see all the moments from the top of the decision. I also stayed because it was fun.

I met people in that line. We were goofballs together, iconoclasts, rebels, nonconformists. We could have been working or jogging or taking care of our kids, all those things normal people do. Not us. We had called a time out. We thumbed our noses at convention. Let the rest of the world march around like puppets, we pulled our own strings. If we wanted to stand in line, ridiculously, for hours on end, then who cared what people thought? We formed a community. We called each other by first names. Someone played games with my daughter. We told jokes, swapped recipes, laughed out loud, hummed melodies. And in the miraculous end, Sylvia purchased tickets for nothing more than a stranger, someone she met while standing in line.

I remember standing in line one hot day at Disneyland. My husband and I waited for Mr. Toad's Wild Ride. We were young and newly married, but most of the people in line were accompanied by children. The line swept past the thirty-minute-wait sign. It was midafternoon, and two women stood near us with two children, both boys, about two and four years old. The younger child happily slept in the arms of the older woman, perhaps Grandma. The four-year-old found no such peace. Miserable from the heat and the wait, tired from an already long day, he headed in that direction all tired children go, toward the perpetual whine.

The boy's mother started to poke him. At first, she spoke softly. "Shut up. Shut up. Stop that." When he didn't stop, she went further. She started to hit him on the head. Her voice got louder. Her comments grew meaner. "You don't deserve to go on this ride. I should have left you home. Baby. Baby."

The rest of us behaved as though we were on an elevator. We shifted our feet and avoided eye contact. We scanned the distant crowd for anybody from home who might be wandering through Fantasyland. We suddenly had to look through our purses or our wallets.

Aching for the boy, angry with the mother, not one of us knew how to help. Not one of us dared to breach the boundaries of privacy that surround families, even when their behavior is public. How far would we have let that situation deteriorate before we intervened? Why did that line dissolve into isolation? The treatment of a child seems of far greater significance than tickets to a Neil Diamond concert, and yet, we couldn't bond around it. It was a profound failure of community.

Once Brad and I and our two daughters were stranded on Christmas Eve at a high-rise motel in Clear Lake, Iowa. We had been on the way to grandparents when a blizzard forced us off the road. We were lucky to get a room. Hundreds of people ended up spending the night in local churches and restaurants.

Wind howled outside. The motel had a pool, but no rental bathing suits except for one paper bikini our body-bashful eleven-year-old wanted nothing to do with. The same two movies rolled around on the television, *Annie* and a sad story of a sick child. Every half hour or so, one of the girls would sigh and exclaim woefully, "Oh, now they're eating chili," or "Now everybody's waiting for Grandpa to get out of the bathroom."

The hotel staff had scrambled to put together a Christmas Eve meal for all their unexpected guests. We stood in line, waiting to be seated. Up and down the hall, bleary-eyed travelers leaned against the walls. Children cried, parents looked whipped, nobody smiled.

"We could sing carols," I said. I repeated it to my flabbergasted family. "We could sing carols. Look at all these miserable people. Why shouldn't we make it fun?"

My eleven-year-old threatened to run away from home. My husband shook his head. Our younger daughter, more willing to give her crazy mother a chance, said, "Okay. You start it, Mom."

By then we were seated at our table. I looked around the silent room. No laughter. No conversation. Everyone stuck hip-deep in disappointment. No one feels like singing, I told myself, as I silently unfolded my napkin onto my lap.

In 1979 Pope John Paul made a visit to Des Moines, Iowa, in response to a farmer who had written and invited him. The Pope was scheduled to land by helicopter at the Living History Farms, a tourist site a mile or so west of the Des Moines city limits. Anticipating large crowds, local officials had blocked off the road, so anyone who wanted to see the Pope had to walk. Probably there were some shuttles or buses for those unable to walk, but I don't remember that. Later, the crowd would be estimated to have been between 300,000 and 350,000. The Interstate was closed and served as a parking ramp for hundreds of buses.

We lived in a western suburb of Des Moines at the time, and I was determined to make the three-mile walk from my home. I could not muster a single friend to go with me, but one did offer to watch my children.

I set out, wearing blue jeans and a T-shirt. It was October, so I must have had a jacket. No blanket, no water, no lunch, no umbrella. Just me, in my walking shoes. After a couple of miles, I came to the road stretching to the Living History Farms, crowded with other pilgrims. Though the sky was overcast, the mood was festive. There were many families with small children, pushing strollers or carrying baby backpacks.

When I got to the farms, I perched on a grassy hillside to await the Pope's arrival. I was surrounded by a sea of people. Many of them had brought blankets, lawn chairs, lunches. Some napped while waiting. I thought of Jesus preaching the Sermon on the Mount and wished someone would show up with multiplied loaves and fishes.

The Pope was late. Where I was situated, I couldn't see the speaker's platform. Eventually, a murmur passed through the crowd that the Pope's helicopter was landing. The clouds parted, the sun broke through, and the crowd grew hushed. Tens of thousands, many seated, as I was, out of sight but not out of hearing, listened as the Pope spoke about the joys and duties of agriculture.

I am not Catholic. I do not share a Catholic's awe of papal authority. But I was moved that day, not so much by the man or the words he spoke, but by the reverence of the crowd. We were a community of seekers, and I felt grateful to belong.

In 2005, on the night we arrived in Rome, Italy, having found the stark convent where we would spend the night and wandered to an internet café to check on things at home, I received an email from my friend Nancy announcing that she had pancreatic cancer. Characteristic of

Nancy's no-nonsense style and prodigious intellect, she had not yet been officially biopsied, but she told all her friends she believed she would have four to six months. She wasn't going to spend it mourning.

As we moved from Rome to Perugia, then to the countryside with day trips into Siena and Orvieto, with their black and white striped marble churches, and finally to the basilica in Assisi, made of rose and cream stone from the Vale of Spoleto, we entered church after church with frescoes, friezes, and murals fierce and frightening: the slaughter of the innocents, crucifixion, judgment day, the sacrifice of Isaac. In every church and cathedral, I slipped a coin into a box, knelt, and lit a candle for Nancy. I was surprised by the comfort I found in this ritual. I did not expect a miracle to occur. I did not think that my kneeling would restore Nancy to health. What moved me were the grooves worn into the kneeling stones where centuries of petitioners before me had cast their longings. I entered that parade of mourners, grateful for the human connection, knowing I was not alone.

Can it be this simple? Sometimes we want to be reminded of our connection to humanity; sometimes we don't. When we need comfort or laughter or joy, we step into the tide. But when we are embarrassed or betrayed or helpless, we collapse into isolation. I don't think we prefer the isolation. The forced isolation of the last two years, during a pandemic, have shown us that isolation breeds despondence and depression. Prisoners are put into isolation as a cruel form of punishment. We collapse into isolation when we don't know what else to do. When our communities fail.

As I write this, Russia is daily pummeling Ukraine, threatening any façade of world order we might have held. A restaurant in St. Paul, Moscow on the Hill, family owned for thirty years by loyal Americans, employers of a diverse staff that includes people from Russia, Somalia, and Mexico, has received hate mail. They've been skewered on social media. This, again! What can be our way out of this maelstrom? We don't appear to be capable of remembering for five minutes that all of creation is our community. Some days, it takes all the hope I can muster to imagine that the long arc of history bends toward justice.

But wait. The Museum of Russian Art in Minneapolis has draped a handmade Ukrainian flag over their sign. A friend has joined a campaign to purchase products online from vendors in Ukraine, asking in the comment section that they not actually send the product as a way of infusing cash into their economy.

Acts of kindness amidst seas of hate. It's not enough, for sure, for sure. But it's not nothing.

Comforter

My husband's brother lay in a hospital bed, dying, though we didn't know it. He was in the last stages of prostate cancer, but he'd been hospitalized with internal bleeding we all thought could be brought under control. Brad went to spend time with him, while I stayed in Minneapolis to deal with the foundation work going on in our basement.

I wouldn't say that my husband Brad and his brother Don had a close relationship. They were born ten years apart. Don had been a superstar athlete in a small-town arena, idolized by his younger brother. When Don left for college, Brad was only seven.

Still, in later years, they treated each other with respect. Don lived in Omaha, taught junior high social studies until he retired. Never married, he lived in a bachelor apartment, and later, when his mother moved to assisted living, he moved into the family home. He was surrounded by a large extended clan, two sisters and their families, a plethora of cousins. Brad and I lived with our two daughters in Minneapolis, no other family within hundreds of miles, so we didn't get home that often.

During his hospital stay, Don wanted either Brad or one of his sisters to sit near the bed where he could see them. One day, Brad sat vigil while neither sister was in the room. Don was hooked up to tubes and monitors, his belly swollen from fluid retention, his head covered with a pale chemo fuzz. Brad, a tall, lean man, blond hair tipped with gray, close-cut white beard, sat, legs crossed. Both men wore glasses, the only physical similarity between them.

"When you were little," Don began, "and you had a nightmare and woke up scared, what did you do?"

Brad sat up, attentive. "What did you do?"

Don said, "I pulled the covers over my head to hide." Then, after a long pause, "That's what I'd like to do now."

Brad placed his hand on Don's. "What about you?" Don asked.

Brad said, "I'd go find Mom."

There were many more moments of tenderness between them in Don's final two weeks. I was also present during the last week of Don's life, and he spoke to all of his family with love, grace, and generosity. Once he decided to go into hospice care, we hovered over his bed, aware that when they started sedating him for pain, we wouldn't have him with us in the same way.

"You've been the best brother," Brad said.

"How would you know?" Don quipped. "I'm your only brother."

The morning came when Brad and I had to tell Don goodbye. We needed to drive to Minneapolis to take care of things at home, and no one could predict how long Don might linger. He was heavily sedated, but the nurses told us he could hear us even if he couldn't respond. We told him we loved him. Then Brad leaned over and whispered into his ear, "Go find Mom."

Don died that night in his sleep.

Death is mysterious. Long as we can, we try to outwit and outrun it, perhaps to our own detriment. When the doctors were still focused on fixing him, Don suffered a lot of pain. His bowel had shut down, and while the medical professionals hoped it would wake up, they couldn't risk too much sedation.

I just got off the phone with a dear friend whose husband is hospitalized. He's been struggling with two separate metastatic cancers. He underwent emergency surgery for a bowel obstruction. Now he has pneumonia and a fever, and his heart rate is dangerously spiking. No one—yet—is talking palliative care. My friend is miserable and exhausted, second-guessing every move as if she could fix this, if only she makes all the right decisions or is caring enough.

This is hard stuff. Loss is the price of our loving. But suffering? Do we prolong it with our inability to accept mortality?

Religions have imagined an afterlife to assuage our fears, the wrenching thought of separation. But some of us are neither willing nor able to suspend our disbelief.

The comfort of a loving mother is a great image. Held and cushioned. Soothing. Go find Mom. I love the verbs in that line. Go and find. It's time now. Don't be afraid. Millions have done it before you. Seek comfort. Sleep.

Salvador Dalí and Me

I stood in the cordoned off doorway to a small bedroom exhibit. Above the bed hung a tapestry displaying a copy of one of Salvador Dalí's most famous works, *The Persistence of Memory* or, more popularly, melting clocks.[1] Three distorted clocks drooped over a branch, a table edge, and a mound of white. We were at the Dalí museum, high in the Pyrenees above Barcelona, in the town of Figueres. The story our guide told is that Dalí and his wife, Gala, entertained friends on their patio on a warm day. Gala and the others went into town, leaving the dishes behind. As Dalí waited for their return, a seemingly interminable passage of time, the Camembert cheese melted. Dalí's realization—that time is variable depending on the context—resulted in this painting, a meditation on Einstein's burgeoning theories of the relativity of space and time. In the science-driven twentieth century, ever pressing for more exactitude, melting clocks caused quite a stir. As for me, I was moved, for I, too, have had occasion to reconsider time.

I am sitting in the lobby of the women's unit at the hospital where I underwent chemotherapy for ovarian cancer. The space, appointed with teal couches and a circular chandelier that falls like crystal rain, has not changed in the two years I've been coming here. A lab technician draws blood, a procedure that takes only seconds. I will have to wait several hours for the results. A nurse calls my name and walks me to an examining room. Blood pressure, weight: stable. I undress from the waist down, cover myself with a sheet, and prop on the edge of the stirruped table to wait for Dr. Gibbons.

We greet each other warmly. Stocky in build, longish blond hair, a doctor's lab coat, and impractical shoes. Today, wedge heels. She examines me vaginally. Everything looks and feels normal.

When she asks how I am doing, I say, "I'm adjusting to a different relationship with time."

She sits. "Tell me about that," she says.

We humans are fanatics about measuring time: day, night, phases of the moon, seasons, when the groundhog shows his face. Over time, we have pressed for more precision. The caesium atomic clock used to be our most accurate timekeeper, off by one second every 9,192,631,770 cycles of microwave radiation. Recently a team of German scientists perfected a clock a hundred times more accurate, an optical single-ion clock that works by measuring the vibrational frequency of ytterbium ions as they oscillate back and forth. This clock won't gain or lose a second in several billion years, creating a flurry of research to redefine the second.

Yet, as Dalí discovered on the day the cheese melted, we do not experience time as a precise measurement. Time, to us mortals, is not stable at all, but a shapeshifter, long and elastic when we are young, hurling down an icy slope as we age. Time crawls for children on the last day of school, pregnant mothers who are overdue, people stranded in an airport. It races for exam takers, lovers on vacation, working parents. Think of it this way. Time, as we live with it, is more like a liquid than a solid. If you poured it from a pitcher, it might drip slowly or gush like a waterfall, dependent on many variables: the amount within the container, the angle of the tilt, the height from which it's poured. Even the dictionary is equivocal about time: a moment, a stretch, a span of existence, an era.

If you are a cancer patient waiting for lab results, time oozes from that pitcher like crystalized honey from a jar. On the same day that I had this conversation with my gynecologic oncologist, I learned that my CA125 was elevated. The CA125 is a blood marker that measures antigens, and an elevation for an ovarian cancer patient almost certainly indicates a recurrence. The average life span after a recurrence is three to five years. A single flutter of a hummingbird's wing. During the following months, I struggled to define my relationship with elusive time. I needed a new definition not only of the second, but of minutes, hours, days, and should I be so lucky, years.

I meet a friend for coffee. My friend suffers from mental illness and severe back pain. She hauls around several pillows to enable sitting; sometimes she lies on the floor. A handsome woman with dense, curly gray hair, she is wearing black pants and a stylish sweater. We sit in facing leather armchairs, the air redolent with ground coffee beans. Whirrs and spurts of grinders and emulsifiers. She spends several minutes adjusting her supportive pillows. Once she is settled, her first words to me are, "You and I have lost our innocence."

"Yes," I say. "We have."

"It helps to know someone understands."

Denial of mortality is no longer available to either my friend or me. We are burdened with awareness. Like Captain Hook, hounded by a ticking clock. At the same time, neither of us has a definitive harbinger of death. We could both live a long time.

I have tried to talk about what it's like to live with this uncertainty. Most people respond by saying, "No one knows what will happen tomorrow." While this may be true, before I was diagnosed with cancer, I lived with assumptions I can no longer make. My problem is not that I don't have knowledge, but that I have too much. Should I, for instance, undertake a long-term writing project? Does it make sense to develop a five-year plan for dealing with our old house? Knowing he was facing imminent death, Oliver Sacks pledged to "live in the richest, deepest, most productive way" he could. But not facing imminent death, it's difficult to shoulder that intensity. Can I live, perhaps for years, feeling that I must not waste a single minute?

Moving in and out of the threat of death is a peculiar time-warping experience.

Recently I participated in a drumming workshop. While others learned complicated rhythms on African djembes, I was instructed to keep a steady clave beat on a dunun, a small double-headed drum that rests on its side and is played with a stick. Bells clanked out a steady four beats, djembes flickered through complicated patterns, and my job was to hold on to an offbeat clave rhythm, three steady beats followed by two quick beats. Against the competing rhythms, I found it difficult to keep time.

There are many competing rhythms in life. A friend once remarked that she knew she was middle-aged because her mother wanted more time with her than she was willing to give, and she wanted more time with her children than they were willing to give. During chemotherapy, a friend who has a passion for organization wondered if I felt compelled to declutter. Others suggested I compile photo albums. My neighbor, faced with a fatal diagnosis, walked his wife through their financial management. Against all these potential demands, how does one plan a day? How can I find my rhythm, convert the noise of my life into music? What is my way of keeping time?

What does it mean, anyway, to keep time? What prison or container would hold it? The strongest central tower of a castle is called a keep, but even that could not prevent time slipping away.

We North Americans complain and brag about how busy we are, never enough time. We treat time as a commodity, largely unconscious of any option other than a fast-moving treadmill.

While in college, our daughter spent a year studying in Spain. In Seville, she experienced a different mode of time. At first, she would phone and say, "They don't do anything here. When they have siesta, they just sit around." By the end of the year, she admired her new friends' commitment to family, the spontaneity of friendly get-togethers that didn't require a juggling of calendars, and she began to wonder why we Americans are always in such a hurry. When she came home, she had to readjust to our way of life.

"Mom," she said, on the phone from Madison during her senior year of college. "I'm lonely. I live with three roommates, and I like all of them. But I never see them."

"It's exams," I said, trying to help.

"No, even before that. They're busy. We're all running in separate directions."

"What are they busy doing?"

"School," she said. "Activities." Then, she paused. "I'd be willing to give up a meeting if we could just have dinner together, but they don't think it matters."

She sounded forlorn, and I didn't know what to tell her. Should I have said, my friends don't think it matters either? Some comfort.

I think about this now and wonder: If we spend time reactively, wouldn't it be better to use it intentionally? But constant intention is wearing and creates its own pattern of anxieties.

I am on the phone with my friend Ruth. She has bladder cancer that has metastasized to her bones. She has undergone chemo and targeted radiation. Her tumors have shrunk, but they are still present. She feels fine, but she will be dead in six months.

"I saw some shoes last week," she says. "I wanted them, but they were expensive. I don't know if I'm going to live long enough to get any good out of things."

"I know," I say. "I wanted to buy a knitting needle kit. Every time I buy new needles, it costs another $20. But the kit costs $200. That's a long-term investment."

Then, I confess, "Ruth, I bought the needle kit."

"Did you?" she says. "I bought the shoes."

We laugh.

"But," she says. "You know what? The shoes hurt my feet, so I don't wear them."

Then we laugh harder.

My neighbor who recently died of cancer wrote his own obituary. A man of wry wisdom, he wrote, "preceded in death by billions of others." I chuckled and applauded this invitation to a perspective that I knew was hard-won.

Eventually, I learned to take consolation in the recognition of my mortality. Like my neighbor, I caught glimpses of a long view of time, life stretched before and beyond my brief existence. Time immemorial.

I sat often on our patio, surrounded by garden, watching the occasional hummingbird, a bevy of squirrels, lilting butterflies, scurrying chipmunks, and way too many rabbits for a gardener's ease, thinking we are the same, you and I, tissue and sinew and bone, vulnerable to disease and marked for an eventual death. I loved everything with a palpable ache, even the damn rabbits, and the green hostas and spiky lilies and lacy astilbes, and I found it comforting to think that I would return to the earth, out of which a living elm or penstemon or geranium might arise.

When I was told that I had a recurrence of cancer, one tiny part of my brain was relieved. I wrote in my journal: I can stop waiting for the other shoe to drop. I could get busy dying.

My CA125 continued to rise for two months then mysteriously dropped. Eight months after the initial threat of recurrence, after many blood tests and several CT scans, my oncologist declared that the recurrence was false. The scare, the holding our breath, the acclimatization, then a reprieve. My husband and I wanted to be elated, but we were exhausted.

Months later, he and I talked about this period.

"You made a rapid transition," he said.

"What did that look like?"

"You were preparing to die. Your priorities shifted."

"What about you?"

"I couldn't get there."

We dwelt on different planes of the space-time continuum, and it took some work to re-enter each other's orbit.

Once you become aware that your Camembert cheese is melting, you cannot unlearn what you know. But surprisingly, you can adjust. I got better at simultaneously accommodating the threat of death and claiming life. I bought the knitting needles. I rest in the long view of time, but I practice residing in this day only. When my husband hugs me in the morning, I tuck my face into the bend of his neck and breathe in his scent. I listen to Rutter's *Requiem* and weep. I marvel at the iridescent sheen of a Japanese beetle as I pluck it off my garden zinnias and dump it in a killing jar. I go to movies and read books and eat pasta and walk with my friends. I linger over pictures of my daughters as infants, toddlers, middle and high schoolers, thinking, along with every other parent, where did the time go? I sail into happiness with my grandchildren, pushing them high and higher in swings that bear them to the illimitable sky.

INTERSECTIONS of MEMORY and TRUTH

My Earliest Memory

I am three years old, standing at my desk in the corner of our living room. Hot pink walls shimmer in the afternoon sun. Over the window, a filmy white curtain undulates like a clean sheet when my mother rolls it over the bed. A gold-framed mirror decorated with painted flamingoes hangs above a red upholstered couch. Across the room squats a matching red chair. I sometimes sleep in the chair, my head resting on one wide arm, my legs thrown over the other, my body curved in an immovable hammock. When I get up from a nap, the backs of my legs are imprinted with spirals from the pattern in the upholstery. Blond end tables stand guard at either end of the couch, stepped like stairs held high on rickety stilts. One table holds a lamp with a glass base that doubles as a fishbowl. All the fish die. Crammed next to the stove with the mica-chipped eyes looms a dark-stained upright player piano. The guts are ruined, so it doesn't play by itself anymore, but my dad can play tunes on it with one hand. People say he plays by ear. I think that's funny because he never puts his ear on the keys. There's a high-heeled table that my parents received as a wedding gift. A starched green doily forms a collar around a second lamp, the base a rearing black ceramic horse topped by a red rectangular shade fringed in black. On either side of the horse, like bookends, hunker two planters shaped like horses' hooves. All the plants die. Gramp's rocker is in the room, too, along with a cherrywood secretary, the shelves displaying family photos. When the front is pulled down and resting on its hinges, I can see cubbyholes full of papers, Dad's pocketknives, a pair of wire-rimmed glasses. The desk smells like oil and leather, like my daddy's neck above his collar. Against another wall stands Gramp's old library table with encyclopedias lined up on the shelf under it and a Victrola on top. Sometimes my dad makes recordings. He lays a flat black disc on the turntable and plugs in a squawky microphone. My mother giggles and says, "I don't know what to say," and we take turns talking. I don't say much, but my brothers sing a cowboy song that starts, "My home's in Montana, I wear a bandanna . . ."

On the day I am three, I am standing at the desk my dad made for me. He fashioned it from plywood, set in a little drawer on the right-hand side, glued slate on top. I don't have a room in this house; I sleep in a crib in the corner of my parents' bedroom. My brothers share a double bed in the other bedroom, wedged between a tall wardrobe and a gun cabinet that holds Dad's hunting rifles. This desk in this corner is the only space that is mine. I stand in the corner, and I say to myself, "I am three years old. This is my desk. I will never forget."

Memory Thefts and Transplants

The girl joins her father to watch the Nebraska sun set. His right elbow is crooked, his arm resting on the corral fence. She moves to his left side, squeezes between him and Jack, an old black hound dog. She centers her gaze between the split rails of the fence. Slides her fingers into his palm. His large, rough hand folds around hers. She turns her head to look at him. He tongues a matchstick from one corner of his mouth to the other without touching it with his hands. His skin glows like a new penny. His overalls pockets carry Juicy Fruit gum, her favorite, a pocketknife to remove splinters, a brown leather coin purse with a gold snap-clasp. His wire-rimmed glasses sparkle in the sun's slanted rays. The pith helmet on his head sits like a lampshade, the crown soiled with sweat. She can stand on the steel-hardened toes of his work boots, laced with long, square-edged sinews of cowhide, while he dances her around a room. Now, they do not speak. She turns her head in the twilight. Together, they watch the sky.

*

Like my father, Isaac Newton must have spent a lot of time looking at the sky. Newton was a lackluster student at Cambridge University. The classics didn't interest him. Alchemy, emerging theories of mechanical science, and biblical prophets did. He floated on a path of sunlight from an open casement window to an unmade cot in the corner of his room. Out of that observation, he designed his most famous experiment, involving two sheets of paper with pinholes and two prisms, proving that white light is dispersed into homogenous colors. Even that might not have happened had fate not intervened. The plague forced the shutdown of the university for two years, and Newton retired to a solitary laboratory in the small village where he grew up. At the age of twenty, Newton trusted his vision of the sky, the relationship of moons and planets in elliptical orbit, and he developed his laws of motion.

Everything that seems at rest stays at rest; everything that seems in motion stays in motion—unless acted upon by an outside force. See how he finds a loophole. He is writing laws, intractable and pervasive, but something warns him. Some star flickers in an inexplicable way, some shaft of light bends in an unexpected direction, and Newton, in his private laboratory provided by the intervention of the plague, adds a qualifier: *seems*.

I wonder now when I first became aware of the hedge of *seems*. When did I first suspect that things are not necessarily what they appear to be? The earth looks flat but isn't. Caterpillars seem destined to die as fat, hairy worms but don't. My hand looks solid but is instead a mass of quivering atoms. Set your foot on a log, and it may open into the jaws of an alligator. Failures turn out to be stepping stones. Dreams fade once the hand closes on them.

When I was four or five, I awoke thirsty on Christmas Eve. I stepped into the small living room of our home, startling my father, who scurried out from behind the Christmas tree. The room was draped in electrical cord and triangulated by three silver-coned movie lights. Dad filmed every Christmas morning with an 8mm camera, the forerunner of the modern video camera. Moving pictures but no sound. Designed for outdoor use, the camera required elaborate lighting to film indoors. Dad rigged the whole apparatus every year to film movies that turned out more or less identical, except the kids grew older. Mom always got a purse. I got a doll. My brothers unwrapped cowboy gear and cars and trucks. Miraculously, on films recorded year after year, we all seem surprised.

On that Christmas Eve, I was not surprised to find my father stringing movie lights. Yet, when I asked Dad what he was doing, he said his back hurt and he was lying under a heat lamp. "Can I lie down with you?" I asked. Dad rotated one of the movie lights on its tripod, and he and I lay under it. I remember looking up at the bright light, the sun captured on a stick, and nestling into my dad's shoulder, where I must have fallen asleep, and he carried me back to bed. For years, I did not understand why my dad told me that particular lie. It occurs to me only now that he must have been placing gifts under the tree, not stringing camera lights. Whose innocence was he protecting, his or mine?

My father's life is lost in the hedge of *seems*. My early memories of my father have fallen away from me like a distant echo. Later experiences, overheard snatches of conversation, impressions from other people, gleaned fragments of knowledge I have uncovered like a spy on a mission have given me a more complex picture of my father but have robbed me of my memories. I remember how I remembered him, but I am no longer sure if what I remember is fact or what I created.

I know that before I was born, Dad had been a farmer. His lifelong habit of watching the sky must have grown out of the wariness of a man dependent on the weather. He farmed with his father on leased land because my grandfather, an immigrant Englishman, refused to pay land tax to the American government. Their enterprise was an amalgamation of science and superstition; they planted by the phases of the moon but also owned the first motorized tractor in the county. Dad's particular role was to service and repair the succession of tractors: a McCormick Deering, Fordson, Cletrac, and Caterpillar. My father's mechanical aptitude was legendary in the farming community; he could repair anything on wheels. Once, he hand-built a beet loader, improving on the current design, and patented his invention. When I was a child, our yard was littered with Dad's rusty machines, skeletal monuments of the past.

After Gramp died, my father sold half the machinery to give my grandmother an income to live on. With limited equipment and without my grandfather to manage the business end of farming, my father failed. "He had no backbone," my mother said, only one in a series of remarks she recited like a litany: "he was unlucky," "hailed out seven years in a row," "a hard worker but he didn't know how to deal with people." With a sigh, she added the summation, "His whole life was almost and not quite."

I was born when my father was forty-one years old, when the heyday of his life had already ended. He never stopped yearning for land, though he never found a way to realize his dreams. I knew none of this in my early childhood. He was my daddy, big and kind, his low voice singing in my ear.

I am three years old, and my family is Christmas shopping. We are in Scottsbluff, a town twenty-five miles west of our house in the country. We don't own our house. We have electricity, but no running water. Our address is Rural Route #1, and the town we are attached to is a small town on the North Platte River in the panhandle of Nebraska. Scottsbluff, this big town, has stoplights and a Montgomery Ward store and a Sears. Snow falls in lazy, lacy hunks. The clusters sting my cheeks and tickle my tongue. Colored bulbs stretch diagonally across the intersection. A plastic reindeer rides the corner post. The light turns green, and Dad bends over and scoops me up in his arms. He's wearing his town hat, and his neck smells of aftershave. I turn my face into the warmth above his collar. I look over his shoulder at other kids, the lights, the snow, the fake Santa ringing a bell with paper poppies bleeding in his white mitten, and I stretch my hand like a queen to her subjects.

While Newton gazed at the sky, he must have encountered the wandering stars. He watched out his open casement window and observed that certain stars appeared to travel backward, a little slip, a momentary zigzag in the wrong direction. Newton would have known this was an optical illusion. Newton would have listed this phenomenon in his category of *seems*. Newton would have explained it to a younger cousin or a later student in his classroom as a mirage created when the earth catches up to another planet against a backdrop of distant stars.

Newton's knowledge of the wandering stars did not prevent him from making a few zags of his own. He suffered from fatigue and depression throughout his life, possible symptoms of chronic mercury poisoning contracted from three decades of alchemical research. Like other alchemists, Newton was determined to isolate the philosopher's stone. Not a stone at all, but a liquid hatched in a beaker called the philosopher's egg, this elixir of life was believed to transform any common substance to the purest gold, infinite wealth. Newton, like other alchemists, was not so concerned with the gold product. He wanted to harness the miracle of transformation, to understand the mysteries of birth, death, and life. Like other alchemists, he was doomed to disappointment. Like my father, he chased an illusion no more tangible than the ghostly zag of a wandering star.

When I was eight, my dad went through a transformation none of us would ever understand. One day the father I knew went away, and some other man showed up in his place. This man's mouth twisted, and his voice got big. My mother said, "Dad's not himself," and I believed her. I was afraid of the stranger who was my father.

One bad morning I wake up early. I sleep in a crib in the corner of my parents' bedroom. I'm too big for a crib, but there's no other space for me in this house. I sleep with my back to the wall because the scary monster that lives under my bed comes out at night and haunts the space between their bed and my crib. A Sunday School plaque hangs on the wall above my head. Tan, with white carved words, *Jesus loves me*. Atop Grandma's old dresser sits Mom's green plastic jewel box and a tiny wooden chest. Inside the miniature drawers are locks of baby hair wrapped in waxed paper, mine and my two older brothers'. Clothes hang on a rod that juts from the back of the door. There's just room enough for Dad to stand at the foot of the bed and take off his overalls. He hangs them on a hook on the wall. This bad morning, I hear noises. Light streaks under the drawn window shade. My dad is sitting up in bed, and he is spanking my mother. His face is twisted and mean. She is turned over his knee. He hits her with his flat hand, more than once. I remember it now in slow motion, his hand moving through the air as big as the wing of an airplane. I cannot see myself in the picture, but I hear my mother crying.

My father's slide into mental illness lasted only a brief period in my family's history. For my mother, it was a temporary detour, hardly consequential against the larger orbit of their life together. For me, it was a defining period of my childhood. Perhaps two years after this episode, after other violent outbursts, after many paranoid accusations against my mother, after desperate jaunts to various doctors around the region, my father seemed to trade his emotional unrest for physical deterioration. His hands shook; his feet shuffled. He remained passive and gentle unless he tried to handle the pressures of a job; then he would again become restive and accusatory. Eventually, he didn't work, and my mother took up the burden of support. When I was sixteen, Dad was diagnosed with Parkinson's Disease. Almost nine years had passed since his episodes of violence, and we never knew whether they were related to his declining physical health. He died a week before my thirtieth birthday.

Once when my mother, my brothers, and I tried to talk about Dad, we sounded as if we were four separate sky gazers expounding theories on a wandering star. My mother, who clung to the clarity of medical diagnosis, claimed that Dad was a strong and wonderful man who got sick. My oldest brother, already launched and out of the house when the worst trouble started, shrugged and said, "He was a hippie before his time." My other brother, the middle child, who shared my mother's practicality and resented the hardships Dad's limitations imposed on her, declared that Dad was a stubborn son of a bitch when he was living and a stubborn son of a bitch the day he died. I, the youngest, the only daughter, the one who rode high in his arms like a queen and then awoke to witness his madness, could not find a definitive answer. I am undone by the unsolved mysteries of transformation. I observe his trajectory across my life, and I cannot distinguish the true path from the phantom zag.

Newton observed the sky, the ordinary sun and stars, the planets and the moon. He studied the constellations and let the winged bow of Orion carry him further and further out into speculations beyond his immediate sphere of observation. Beyond the then-known world of science. He looked at the sky and imagined a bold theory of the universe. He must have known that it could all blow up in his face.

When I approach the past, I am in danger of spontaneous combustion. My mother would have liked to perform a memory transplant on me, cauterize the gashing wounds and replace them with sweet dreams. She interpreted my resistance to a happy childhood as an act of deliberate defiance, and she took it personally. I wanted to help her out. I wanted to be a good daughter. But like Newton, my vision of the sky is all I have.

Some years ago, I traveled to western Nebraska to visit my mother, who lived in the small town we moved to when I was ten. Together we drove to Ordville, the army munitions complex west of Sidney, where my father worked during the fifties. It was a late September day, 95 degrees on the car thermometer, the hills brown from a summer drought. The sky wobbled in the heat, and dust billowed across parched roads.

We turned off the dirt road into the ruins of a ghost town. I was surprised to find row after row of abandoned government housing, stucco units painted green, peach, or yellow, fading and chipped, weeds crowding what must have once been well-tended yards. I did not know that people had lived out here, having assumed that because my father commuted, everyone did.

"Dot and Ken lived here," my mother said. "Addie, too. We had our house all picked out after we got out of farming."

By the time I was old enough to remember, my Aunt Addie lived in Sioux Villa, a low-rent development of government row houses on the west edge of Sidney. My Uncle Ken and Aunt Dot lived in a post–World War II housing development named Sky Manor. Though the houses were small and prefab, my mother dreamed of owning one because they were modern, with picture windows and low ceilings. Influenced by his work at Ordville, my uncle built a bomb shelter in his backyard.

"What happened?" I asked my mother. "Why didn't you ever move here?"

"Dad couldn't pass the physical. They said he had a hernia, so we moved into that little house out by Degraw School."

"Then how did he get the job later?"

"He went to a specialist in Omaha. Turned out he didn't have a hernia. So, he came back out here, and they hired him. Only by that time, we were already settled."

As we drove across the road toward the abandoned cafeteria and ramshackle warehouses, the old school and officers' quarters, my mother talked about how much she would have loved this life, living close to family, chatting with neighbors over linked picket fences, playing canasta or Monopoly on weekends. On a now-dry field, there had been a communal garden where everyone gathered to work in the evenings, and Mom saw herself picking beans and pickling beets and canning corn with a tribe of young women, their children romping together in open fields. While her voice carried her over the longed-for past, I tried to imagine my father here. The man I knew was intensely private, craved land of his own, needed the space offered by a wide, ambivalent sky. He was people-shy and reticent. He balked at the idea of moving to town long after his health prevented him from farm labor. I could not imagine him abiding this kind of communal living. I began to wonder if he had actually failed that physical. Not for the first time, I marveled at the apparent mismatch of my parents' personalities and how little they may have understood each other.

Deciding not to venture back the way we had come, my mother and I drove north and then east to wind our way back to the highway. Up over a ridge, on what looked like a dead-end road, we chanced upon fields of bunkers, regimental rows of grass-covered concrete-poured cones stretching for miles, farther than we could see.

"This is where they stored the bombs," my mother said matter-of-factly.

We hushed our voices, awed by the impact of history, the ghostly visitation of a past war still leaving its imprint on this abandoned stretch of western prairie. Each bunker had a small wooden door and a single ventilation stack. My father labored here—during what my mother considers the best years of their lives because he brought home a steady paycheck—stacking heavy crates of ammunition and bombs, in a tight enclosed space with no windows to even hint of sky. He must have found it intolerable.

I have since read that among those who worked in post–World War II munitions storage facilities, there is a high percentage of autoimmune and neurological illnesses, including Parkinson's Disease. Is it possible that my father was exposed to some chemical that created havoc with his nervous system, manifesting itself first in his uncharacteristic displays of anger and then in an incurable disease? Was he like Newton, a sky-gazing, mechanically oriented loner, poisoned into depression by the by-products of his labors? Or was he simply ill-equipped for adult life, having lived too long under the thumb of a stubborn, domineering father? What happened, what went wrong, to reduce his promise to almost and not quite?

After his bouts of anger subsided, my father and I grew close. He loved books, as I do, and music and beauty and impractical things. Although he did not attend my high school activities, every day at noon I walked home and sat down to a lunch my father prepared. I do not remember a single conversation or even if we talked. Often, I am sure, we shared the silence, and I felt easy in his presence. Many days, I spent the rest of my lunch hour playing the piano, my father reading in a chair.

Once, after I had married and moved away, I was called home because Dad was hospitalized. His throat muscles refused to work, and he could not swallow food or medication. He could not move or respond, although he was fully conscious. For the duration of Dad's hospitalization, when we believed he had only a few days to live, I served as his interpreter. Barely able to whisper, his voice weak and clogged with phlegm, he breathed syllables into my ear, and I translated his breath into words. "Could you raise his bed?" I asked the nurses. "He wants us to go on home," I explained to my mother. To Dr. Post, the rural physician who spent his midnight hours scouring medical journals for information to save my father's life, I apologetically murmured, "Dad wants you to call a specialist at the university hospital."

Now, I am still Dad's interpreter, only the task has grown more complicated. Not here to defend himself or illuminate the puzzles of his life, I am left to sort out for myself who he was. From broken shards, I assimilate and discard, building myself a man.

The man I remember loved the sky. His theme song might have been "Don't Fence Me In," and it would have been sung by Bing Crosby. He never drank, never smoked, peppered his everyday speech with *hell* and *damn*, and had little use for small talk. With only an eighth-grade education, he took correspondence courses in engineering from the University of Nebraska. He invented a few things, farm implements, gadgets, and owned at least one patent. He never made much money. He couldn't bear to let a thing go, rigging up an outdoor stand for our used Christmas trees until they turned brown and brittle. Once, unable to manage the buttonholes of a new shirt with trembling fingers, he cut off all the buttons so that he could remove the shirt and lie down without wrinkling it. He was a hunter who would not shoot after sundown or aim his rifle at a sitting bird. He knew plumbing, wiring, carpentry, and auto repair and put all those skills to use around our home. After years of illness, in response to a question I asked about the best years of his life, he insisted that every day is a good day. He lied to protect me at least twice, once about the purpose of movie lights and once when he studied his symptoms at the local library, noted the word *incurable*, and kept the diagnosis to himself for six years. He was fascinated by technology, filming the Apollo moon landing from the snowy television. He kept a scrapbook of historical clippings and filled tiny memo pads with tidbits of information: prices of bread, the world's largest volcano, the location of Robidoux Pass. Although he didn't read music, he wrote a few songs and believed, at age forty, that he could abandon farming and become an overnight songwriter. One of his songs, "Sweetheart, Say You'll Be Mine," was published by a vanity press, and our family holds all ten copies. The sheet music is mint green with a purple silhouette of a man and woman kissing against the moon and stars of a nighttime sky.

In Pursuit of Magic

Adults lie to children all the time. Take, for instance, Santa Claus. How about Band-Aids? Let Mommy kiss it, it will feel better. They didn't mean it, Honey. Maybe next year we'll go to Disneyland. Of course Bootsie is in cat heaven. When you grow up, you're going to be beautiful. Grandma loves watching you blow bubbles while standing on one foot. What do you mean, wasn't listening? I heard every word you said.

While tearing ivy from the brick of our house, my stepdad accidentally crushed two of my daughter's personally selected, hand-planted impatiens plants. "Never mind," my mother said. "We'll just stick a few of these other plants in there." Something, maybe conscience, pricked me, but I ignored the prick. Mom and I transplanted two pink impatiens, replacing the two broken fuchsia ones. Pink was as close as we could get, and Mom said she'd never notice.

My daughter walked off the school bus, sashayed around to the side garden, and entered at the back door, furious. "What did you do to my flowers?" Of course, I had to confess. She forgave her grandpa immediately. Me, she stiffed with resentment.

At bedtime, she began to relent. "I didn't think you'd do it, Mom."

"Do what?" I asked.

"Lie like that."

The lie got to her more than the deed we tried to cover up. We know lying works like that, and still, we do it. Why do we lie to our children? We tell ourselves it's because they have a right to childhood. We say we're protecting them, guarding their innocence. That is probably the biggest lie of all.

Let's face it. Adults lie to children for their own sakes. We lie to protect our innocence. We lie because we need to see the glow in a toddler's eyes when St. Nick jingles a bell. We lie because our children carry us back to a time we never knew for ourselves but exists in our imaginations. We lie because we can't bear the truth; it puckers our lips like a persimmon.

I don't remember believing in Santa Claus, though it's likely that I did. I have two older brothers who no doubt set me straight, like they did with the Easter Bunny. What is true is that my family silently agreed to play the Santa Claus game.[1] My parents withheld our presents and placed them under the tree after we went to bed on Christmas Eve. Mom would wake us in the morning by yelling, "Santa Claus came." We'd pile out of bed, feigning surprise and awe at the pile of packages glittering under the bubble lights on the tree, mirrored in the hanging tinsel, wrapped in traditional red and green paper or the Sunday comics, tied with curly ribbons. Such bounty and enchantment! We continued this tradition long after we were teenagers.

One year of my life, I slept on the living room couch. I was nine years old. I woke in the middle of the night on Christmas Eve to discover packages under the tree. The tree lights were not on, but moonlight glowed through the window. The scene vibrated with a mystical aura. I arose and walked amongst the presents like a knight who has stumbled on the Holy Grail. I didn't touch anything. I didn't read the tags to see which might be mine. Drunk with mystery and wonder, I eventually lay back down in my makeshift bed on our red upholstered couch and went to sleep. The next morning, when Mom announced that Santa Claus came, I leapt out of bed, feigning surprise and awe, and I did not tell of my late-night venture. Why? I knew I wasn't supposed to have awakened. I knew it wasn't part of our agreed upon game of pretend. Maybe I only wanted to hug it to myself. And maybe, just maybe, I wanted to believe for this singular moment of my childhood that it really was magic.

Dr. Silverman and the Kansas City A's

My two older brothers and I used to play in the neighbor's haystacks, even though we'd been told not to. Our neighbor was also our landlord, but the haystacks were in our yard, so we reasoned that, technically, the haystacks were ours. We lied to our parents, oblivious to the betrayal of our jeans and shirts and socks, littered with clinging wisps of hay. Some years ago, my brother told me that during one of our clandestine romps he launched a weed that struck me in the eye. "It could have put your eye out," my brother said. When I replied that I had no memory of this event, he was incredulous. "I can't believe you don't remember that," he said. "It was one of the worst things that ever happened." I laughed and pointed out things I remembered of far grander proportions, like the time he stabbed his foot, in the back seat of the car, with a hunting knife.

Do you know this theory about memory and rabbits? The rabbit remembers where it has been threatened to avoid danger in the future. This theory relates to Darwin's survival of the species and, of course, Pavlov's dogs. I'm not confident the theory holds, even for rabbits, because Peter Rabbit went straight back to Mr. McGregor's garden, not to mention the persistent munchers of all things green in my city yard. On the surface, it makes sense that we would be more likely to remember highs and lows than the humdrum of everyday existence. And yet, how do we know that what we remember actually happened?

Over a period of fifty years, my husband told a lot of people that his older brother had been drafted straight out of high school by the Kansas City A's, a major league baseball team, but that their father had insisted Don go to college instead. As a little brother, ten years younger, small for his age, and prohibited from sports by badly formed hips that required surgery, Brad suffered a severe case of hero worship for his star athlete brother. Granted, Don was a star in a small patch of sky, but if you grew up during a certain period in a small town in Nebraska, you know that sports (for boys) constituted the singular path to glory. Like Richard Cory, small town athletes glittered when they walked, and Don sparkled brighter than most.

Fast forward over a lifetime of divergent experiences: Don, never married, a junior high civics teacher; Brad, a husband and father, actuary. To my knowledge, the two of them never held a single intimate conversation. They spoke in code, usually around the Nebraska Cornhuskers.

"How do you think the Huskers will do this year?" (*I love you and think of you often.*)

"I don't know. They got that new quarterback." (*I love you and think of you, too.*)

When treatment for advanced prostate cancer failed, Don ended up in the hospital with internal bleeding. During what would prove to be the final days of Don's life, Brad sat at his bedside in the ICU. Don was surrounded by monitors and tubes, fully alert but in pain. The corridor buzzed with hospital activity; the room smelled of sanitizer. Searching for something to say, Brad said, "How come Dad wouldn't let you accept that offer from the A's?"

"What are you talking about?" Don said.

"The Kansas City A's wanting to draft you out of high school."

"Never happened," Don said, in his basso profundo voice, raspy from a lifetime of smoking, softened now by drugs.

Don said that he had played on some community teams, but that was it. He did become a star athlete at Dana College, the only student athlete to letter in basketball, baseball, track, and cross country, but he was never sought by major league—or even minor league—baseball.

Brad was stunned. His respect and love for Don remained untouched, but he could not fathom how he had invented this story, believed it for fifty years, propagated it to a world of friends. "What else?" he said. "How do I know I haven't made up my whole life?"

We hold a certain reverence for what we call facts. At the time I am writing this, our headlines burst with claims of Fake News, casting doubt on the authority of long trusted news sources. Politicians' lies abound, until we are so saturated that we scarcely pay attention. Scientists across the globe testify to climate change, but a cadre of people refuse to believe it, despite evidence many of us would call fact. But even our own memories? How can we trust that we know what we know?

I have a dear friend I'll call Mary. Mary was severely abused as a child and, as a defense, learned to cut off her conscious mind from what was happening to her body. Years later, while married to a good man, when she felt safe and secure, those memories began to raise their heads. She spent years in therapy, coping with the memories bobbing to the surface of her consciousness. We now know that many veterans suffer from PTSD, a form of memory suppression where unbidden memories resurface not as remembered events but as full-blown relived traumatic experience. The cure, for both Mary and other sufferers of PTSD, seems to be moving the memories from the subconscious realm of lived experience into the conscious realm of memory. Memory acts as a filter, in a complicated way, reminding us that the event is in the past.

When I was a child, my parents took me to a dentist I'll call Dr. Silverman. His office was above the dime store. There was another dentist in town, but Dr. Silverman was cheaper. Hardly anyone had dental checkups in those days, fluoride didn't exist, and as a result, I had several large cavities. My parents did nothing, assuming the cavities were in baby teeth that would be replaced. When the cavities in the back teeth of my lower jaw became so large that the nerve was exposed, I wailed from pain and refused to eat. My parents took me to Dr. Silverman, up a steep and narrow staircase, into a room filled with patients, a faint metallic tinge in the air. When it was my turn, I was led into a tiny room, seated in a dental chair surrounded by robotic arms and gadgets, and told to open my mouth. Then the torture began. Dr. Silverman did not use Novocaine. He explained to my parents that the cavities were in molars, permanent teeth, and he would do his best to save them. Because the cavities were so large, he didn't want to waste silver if they couldn't be saved, so first he drilled and filled them with a temporary white substance. Two weeks later, in another prolonged torture session, he removed the temporary filling and replaced it with a semi-permanent dark red cement. Finally, when that proved to hold, he drilled and filled once more, this time with silver. He saved my molars—a laudable feat—but he left me with a lifelong dread of a dental chair.

Let me describe the man. He was big. Not just tall, but big. Hands the size of baseball mitts. He had a thick shock of white hair and a booming voice. The most compelling feature of his persona was his wooden leg. Not just a wooden leg, but a peg leg that made a *clomp-clomp* sound when he strode the hardwood floors of his office.

Except it didn't. Like Brad's memory of Don's missed opportunity, I discovered many years later that Dr. Silverman did not have a wooden leg. He stood firmly on two healthy legs. I invented his wooden leg. Why would I do that?

As a writer, I know the power of metaphor to carry emotional truth. When I was seven, still sleeping in a crib in the corner of my parents' bedroom, I did not turn my back on the empty room out of fear of the hostile creature that lived under my bed. Mary Shelley harnessed ordinary fears to a monster named Frankenstein, only one in a long line of literary concoctions, including Kafka's cockroach.

I gave Dr. Silverman a peg leg. I'm surprised I didn't give him a pirate's eyepatch as well.

Years ago, I returned to the house where I spent the first ten years of my life. Long since abandoned, it had shrunk in size. The yard, which I remembered as spacious, felt fenced in by a tumbledown shed and a root cellar. I could scarcely believe the house sat so close to the dirt road. Where our huge garden used to be and the long clothesline where my mother stood with clothespins clenched between her teeth, there were but a few yards of packed dirt.

In that childhood home, we had a set of encyclopedias that included pages of transparencies of the human body. Starting with a skeleton, you could turn page after page, adding various organs, veins and arteries, muscles, and skin until you created a composite picture. You could study each layer separately, but as they piled up, it became impossible to see the skeleton at the bottom except as a vague outline. With memory, you can keep turning the pages, but it's difficult to go backward. I can remember the way I once remembered my childhood home, but now I have a more recent memory that stands in contradiction. The revisiting of the place crowded out my first memory, so that all that is left is a vague skeletal outline.

At my daughter's high school graduation, which took place on the football field of an inner-city high school, most parents rushed around with video cameras, intent on preserving the event. We did not own a video camera. I literally bumped into another mother, also not filming. When I remarked that we must be the only two parents without cameras, she said, "I think people have a right to re-create their memories as they need to."

I have pondered that insight many times over the intervening years. I used to think memories were fixed, a recording of what actually happened. I knew perceptions of an event could be widely different, depending on all kinds of factors, like the blindfolded men who each handled only a portion of an elephant and were then asked to describe what they felt, but I didn't know, as I do now, that personal memories are fluid. What we remember says more about us than the event that took place. We change over time, so why shouldn't our memories?

I am touched that my brother remembers throwing a weed into my eye as one of the worst things that ever happened, but I hope now that he has new information, the memory will no longer hold guilt for him. Mary hasn't lost her memories; in fact, she has recovered them, but in a way that no longer victimizes her. I gave Dr. Silverman a peg leg, but now I remember that childhood scene with sympathy for the cringing kid in the chair. The scary pirate-figure was only a man doing his job.

Perhaps this is what it means to gain perspective, to climb a little higher on the spiral staircase of our lives. Looking back, we see it all, every twist and turn, but our vantage point changes and, if we are lucky, deepens with compassion.

My Mother, the Liar

My mother said she failed me when she didn't give me a sister. That is one of two, maybe three true things she said to me, the first being that whatever you don't think to worry about will happen. The second, before my wedding day: don't mess with fancy underwear, they just want it off you. Otherwise, my mother was a grand liar with her stories of Heaven and death being a victory. She stood in a long tradition, along with Billy Graham and thumping Baptist pastors of my childhood. Turn your eyes upon Jesus. It will be worth it all. Norman Vincent Peale moved into our magazine rack, and between the church, the Peale, and my mother, I didn't dare complain about anything. Like Gramp's fake oak library table, we were slicked over with a polished veneer.

I'm hearing this now in an Irish lilt, can you hear it? There's maybe a single drop of Irish in me. I come by it naturally, this big imagination, this vision that carries me all the way across oceans. My mother hated this dreaminess in me, afraid I'd turn out wasted like my father. She traveled all the way to Heaven and back on a wisp of longing, but she worried that I'd get lost in stories.

I see her ironing. Bushel basket of wadded-up clothes. Starch crisp and tingling in the air. Shirts, pants, dresses, blouses, endless plaid and stripes and plain. First, haul the water. Then, heat it on the stove. Dump it into three abandoned washtubs. When the wringer sticks, sacrifice your fingers between the slick, doughy cylinders. Bluing keeps the whites white. Clothespins pinch the line. She stands above the ironing board. Her curly hair flies around her face like a cloud of locusts. I sit beside her on a red chair. The torn plastic seat gouges into my thighs as I count, 1, 2, 3. 101, 102, 103. 500. 1,000. I pause, bored.

"Go on," she says, as if she's listening. As if she's not pretending. As if this motherly attention is not a lie.

You think I'm being hard on her. You think that's a lovely thing to do, let a child count out loud for minutes on end. But do you see the apron strings tying me to that chair? Do you know I'd rather be outside, running with my brother, the prairie wind trapped inside our lifted shirts?

She took me with her to her Stanley parties. They were hostess parties at ladies' houses, where I was told not to interrupt her and left alone to navigate a world of nasty children and men lurking in outbuildings. Once I made a child cry, squeezing too hard to make her like me. Another time my mother forgot me, drove away from the curb, and left me gagging on a scream clogged in my throat. At plush rug parties, I sat in a corner, silent. Years later, she would say that even though she had to work, she was with me. I couldn't have left you with a sitter, she'd say. I couldn't have borne it.

She spoke in code. At one of those parties, she asked, "Would you like to pack away my things?" I said politely, "No thank you." Later, on the ride home over bumpy gravel roads, she explained that when she told me to do something in front of a roomful of women, she did not expect me to embarrass her by refusing. "You asked," I said. "You didn't tell me."

"It's not what I say," she snapped. "It's what I mean." And that is the way we lived. I was expected to read her mind.

She lied in other ways, too. You'd never have known how poor we were come Christmas. Bubble lights and tinsel, presents beyond our catalog dreams, smells of turkey roasting and pie. Birthdays, Easter, Valentine's Day, Thanksgiving: the house decorated with crepe paper and fake snow stenciled on windows we'd later scrape with a razor blade.

She was one for making the best of things. Coming home from school, beat up, snot dripping, hard names carved into my skin, she said the only thing she knew and what she told herself, "You shouldn't feel that way." When my father locked himself in the car and refused to come out, when he slapped her against the wall, when he followed us in the pickup, "He's not himself," she said.

She didn't believe in welfare and thought we were lucky to have lived poor. She voted Republican. She said it was the man, not the party that mattered to her. Every man she voted for was Republican except FDR (whom she thought saintly even though he had instituted government safety nets she decried) and Obama, a choice she later recanted. Reading in her presence was an insult. She needed you with her, not ambling away somewhere, your mind in another country. She loved games, especially cards, which I hate. She gloated when she won.

My mother thought she could create a world for people that was better than the one they lived in. All they had to do was step inside her dream, and she had no patience with those who refused. I refused.

In later years, she talked of Heaven. She wanted me to tell her that it would be the way she pictured, all her loved ones reunited. She worried about how it would be managed, she with two husbands, my grandfather with two wives.[1] She asked me because she thought I ought to know, having trained at seminary, and because, compared to my brothers, I am the religious one. She asked me because she wanted me with her, reciting numbers to her from a torn red chair through all eternity. It didn't occur to her that she might get me as I am now, disappointing in my insistence on melancholy and my refusal to play cards.

About Heaven, she asked me, and I gave her what she wanted. I lied to her.

Vaccines

On my afternoon walks, I used to pass a house with an iron lung. The house sat on a corner lot, with turrets and bay windows, brown shake siding, overgrown bushes, and fractured sidewalks. On the ground floor, through a large window, a silver and lime metallic tube glinted in the morning sun.

I speculated endlessly about the mysterious house and its occupants. It once became a topic of conversation at my hairdresser's. A whole row of us, draped in blue plastic, carried on shamelessly with wild imaginings of torture and captivity. Though they are mostly medically obsolete today, in 1959, 1,200 people in the United States lived in iron lungs. Today, two people still rely on them, one a man who has spent nearly seven decades—partially, at first, and then completely—immobilized. I can see myself, age seven, standing outside Bun's Drugs, licking a lollipop, staring at a poster of a child lying in an iron lung, her life cut short and ruined by polio.

My grandmother died from polio, misdiagnosed as a vague paralysis of the throat. My mother was eleven. Years later, when signs of undetected polio showed up in my uncle's gimpy leg and my aunt's misshapen spine, the family figured out Grandma Anna died of polio. Only then, as with most other Americans, did the fear set in. My mother would not let us swim in public swimming pools.

When the first polio vaccine became available, I was in first grade. I attended a one-room country school, and on a school day, all thirteen students were bundled off to town to get a polio shot. Billy, a cousin to the rowdy Schmidt brothers, rode along. Billy had a shock of brown hair that disobeyed every effort of a comb. He'd been staying with his grandmother, and his parents were divorced. He was, for me, a walk on the wild side. Besides, Billy had money, something none of the rest of us had. He took me into the drugstore and bought me a fudgesicle. We plucked penny candy off the shelves in the Five-and-Ten. I don't remember the shot at all.

Some years later, when oral vaccines became available and we had moved to town, I walked across the street and downed a dose of orangish fluid out of a small paper cup. Good measure. Nobody wanted polio.

In our small Baptist community, we were also afraid of the bomb. We mistrusted, even hated, anything Communist. Our suspicions spread to Catholics, too. They wore hats to church long after it was out of fashion. Khrushchev pounded with his shoe on the desk of the United Nations. Shoes and hats; you can see how these associations happen.

My husband, who attended school in a small town not far from Offutt Air Force Base, recalls air raid drills where students practiced hiding under their desks. To doubly protect against the A-bomb, they wrapped their arms over their heads. I lived in the other end of Nebraska, in the forsaken panhandle, where nobody worried that we had anything worth bombing. Nevertheless, my uncle built a bomb shelter. Living in a remote prairie town, he excavated under his house and backyard, poured a twelve-inch-thick concrete shell, lined shelves with canned goods, and talked like a present-day Noah. Watching him build his modern ark, I felt slightly queasy. Either he was nuts or everyone else was, and only time would tell. My mother's argument to her sister was that if a bomb came, she wouldn't want to be the only one left. My aunt shrugged her shoulders and said, "We don't have enough air for you. You should build your own."

Tornadoes put the fear into us, especially since they were acts of God. Lightning, too, but tornadoes were the worst. My brother and I were peacefully seining dirt one day, collecting the softened clay to build a utopian town, when my mother tore into the yard in our beat-up Buick. She screamed at us before the car had come to a stop. TOR-NADO! Unwilling to leave our work behind, we dumped all our dirt in buckets. Mom dragged us each by one arm into the house, where we hid under the red Formica and chrome kitchen table, cradling our buckets of dirt. The wind passed, and we gingerly crawled out. The tornado had missed us, but it tore apart a town to the west. We were later to see far-flung washing machines, flattened houses, and upturned cars. That day, my brother and I were disgusted to have to toss out our dirt, finding it teeming with fat green cutworms.

When my second daughter was born, our older daughter had the good fortune to see her baby sister in the hospital. Siblings were not then allowed, but while I sat with her and her dad in a visitor's room, a nurse came hurriedly through a door. TORNADO. All the mothers, babies, and visitors were lined up facing each other down the second story corridor of a Des Moines hospital until the whistle sounded all clear. Germs and infection were nothing next to the threat of a mighty wayward wind.

I've been in the near miss zone many times for tornadoes, but never in one. The mind grows complacent. I got a reminder some years ago while visiting my mother in Nebraska. A tornado had touched down, skipping large chunks, so that it left its mark like tailor's tacks across a seam of land. A farmer and his wife had both driven separately to town. When they saw the tornado heading toward their farm, each set out in their car to warn the other to take cover. The wife was still en route when the tornado hit. The farmer pulled into the yard in his pickup and leaned down to pick something up off the truck floor; when he sat up again, his house, barn, corral, and all the large trees had vanished. He said, Yeah, he guessed there was a loud noise. His pickup was not scratched. Two days later, someone found a photograph of the farmer's wife and their granddaughter, which had been in a silver frame on the piano. It showed up under the body of a dead horse, three miles away.

My mother used to say that whatever you forget to worry about is what will happen. No polio, no nuclear bomb, no tornadoes in my family, but we had other tragedies. My father was disabled by Parkinson's Disease. A cousin committed suicide. Another cousin was murdered. Another died in a car accident. Another died from spinal meningitis. My forty-nine-year-old cousin died of cancer.

We fend, however we can, against life's vagaries. My daughter is terrified of flying but loves to travel. She plugs into music, holds somebody's hand, takes deep breaths. I have no idea what's in her head, but if it were mine, it would be a prayer or a mantra, something absurd like *let me live, I'll be good, let me live, I'll be good*. Reason goes out the window when up against the indefensible. Some people tell crude jokes. Some cry and wring their hands. Some refuse to say the word, *cancer*, at all. My mother-in-law had some *funny little cells*, underwent radiation, and lived for many years afterward. Rooster's heads, chants in a rainstorm, beads, positive attitudes, deep grieving, whatever gets you through the night. The point is a little inoculation, a daily vaccine against fear.

These days I am overly tender about the clumsiness of our efforts to get by. I cry over Hallmark card commercials. The wafting of a memory, the rustle of a rabbit through a snowbank, the unfolding of a rose, I am scraped raw by precious things on the brink of being lost. The absurdity of life gets to me. I sit listening to a man drone endlessly and nonsensically about how his mother wounded him because she didn't allow him to attend the school of his choice in kindergarten. He is one of those unfortunate people who engenders pity but not real love. He takes up all the space in a room. He's boring and needy, and I wouldn't be listening to him at all if my role as teacher didn't require it. His monologue goes on relentlessly, riding the same topics I've heard time and again, and I am sitting on a big broiling brew of annoyance and compassion. At the same time, I am taking him in like a daily dose of vitamins, bubbling with wicked glee, because on his lapel he wears a button that says, plaintively and absurdly: Can We Talk?

Shards

The notebooks called to me like a beacon across time. I stumbled upon them while packing for a move. Piled, forgotten, on a basement shelf. I dared to look inside. Each page, scrawled in my daughter's loopy prepubescent hand, contained a different list: her stuffed bears' names, all sixty-six of them, a week of the year opposite each name headlined *My Bear-of-the-Week Club*, names she might someday bestow on her children (Pablo, Sean, Dustin, Gabriel, Tony, as if she imagined her family an international community of boys), books and characters in books, places she longed to go.

The most intriguing list was fashioned after *Harriet, the Spy*. One side of the page revealed secret hiding places where she had planted a Gold Bond stamp: behind Mom and Dad's headboard, under the bathroom sink, in a vase in the dining room. On the other side, she recorded observations from each day's spying mission: *Still there, No one saw it,* and alarmingly, *Gone!* She kept this up for days, until she abruptly stopped. Some other interest eclipsed this passion, some other page of her secret life.

On the day I discovered this list, my daughter was seventeen, at least seven or eight years older than her Harriet persona. Nevertheless, I took myself on her patrol around the house. Under the bathroom sink, *Gone!* Behind Mom and Dad's headboard, *Still there!* Wherever I found a long-hidden Gold Bond stamp, I left it. I hoped that she had placed at least one stamp on an object that would stay in the house, mystifying its new owners if they ever ventured to look, say, under the spice drawer in the kitchen.

When I was a child, one of our favorite games was treasure hunt. Either I or one of my brothers, or sometimes our mother if she wasn't too busy, would create the hunt. Those who got to follow the trail waited impatiently in the living room with the curtains drawn shut. I pounded on the piano to pass the time. At last, the hunt-maker would announce that we could begin, and we were off. A slip of paper on the kitchen table might read: Go to the place where Dad stores his tools. Off we raced to the cellar. A note tucked under a screwdriver: Find Jack. Outside to track down our dog, Jack, and see what lay beneath his collar. On and on, to the chicken house, the outhouse, the dilapidated shed, the beet loader, the haystack, the four o'clocks in the garden; nothing was off limits. Some part of the note had to be visible from some angle. That simple rule kept us racing about, lured by the promise of reward, usually no more than a slice of jam and bread or a piece of fruit.

Years later, I tried to re-enact this game with my children, but it was never as exciting for children living in the confines of a city yard as it was for us, tearing all about the countryside. Now, on the day I retraced my daughter's mission for *Harriet the Spy*, I felt the same mounting exhilaration. Losing and finding, losing and finding, I breathed it to myself as I searched for traces of my ten-year-old daughter, evidence beyond my memory, more of her than I had glimpsed at the time. Peering down a hallway of her life, I waited for the open door and wondered what I might find behind it.

I have traveled in the American Southwest. My husband and I collected pottery, even before the Southwest style became trendy. In museums in Albuquerque and Santa Fe, I have stood before glass cases and stared at shards of broken pottery uncovered in excavations. Fragments of civilizations buried by layers of other civilizations, nothing left behind except these traces. Experts study the shards, the intricacy of design, the evenness of the pot, the methods of forming and firing, and from these impressions they make logical guesses about the culture represented. Archaeologists postulate various theories about the sudden abandonment of the Anasazi cliff dwellings, suggesting everything from an environmental disaster to violence or warfare. They tell all that from shards.

Shards are what I have left of my children's childhoods. Grown into accomplished and confident women, they constantly amaze and delight me with who they have become, and yet, I am secretly on the lookout for who they have been. My oldest daughter, a philosophy major who had little taste for Hollywood, once referred to the block-buster movie everyone else had seen as *Titantica*. My husband and I laughed, remembering that years before, during a discussion of the Middle East, she asked, "Is that candy bar named after Beirut?" Our younger daughter (she of *Harriet the Spy*) spent a year studying in Seville as a college student. Struggling with decisions about housing, she wrote, "I've decided that I am a person who at least needs to think she's making her own choices." "No kidding," her dad said, remembering the child who backed herself into a corner of her bedroom and shouted in his face, "You can kill me if you want to, but I'm not wearing that turtleneck."

Once I went on a scavenger hunt of wild proportions. It was, of all unlikely things, a church Halloween party. My husband and I arrived costumed as His and Hers outhouses, entombed in moving cartons we had painted brown, half-moons scrawled on the doors in yellow marker. Quickly we were divided into groups and sent around the city following clues. Out of necessity, the two of us had to abandon our costumes, a lucky break since the hunt took us inside restaurants and shopping centers to pick up pre-planted objects: mints, menus, or matchbooks. Some of the clues were mysteriously written, naming landmark buildings and requiring a bit of historical sleuthing to find the right one and count the number of windows on the south side. I remember that it was raining, and we shrieked and laughed as we piled in and out of a too-small car and slapped through the puddles, dotting our feet and the backs of our calves with mud. We two normally attired participants, my husband and I, were in the company of an orange-wigged clown, a man dressed as a woman, whose balloon breasts kept popping, a pirate with a patch over one eye, and a run-of-the-mill goblin.

On the day I followed my daughter's clues around our familiar house, I wondered what disguise she had been wearing throughout her childhood. I had watched her, it seems, through the slats of a split rail fence. I only thought I saw the whole picture, a child entire in her pursuit of friends, her gift for funny language (she once complained about having to play *patrifying* songs at her piano lessons, like *pomp and circumference*), her incontestable will, but it turned out these were mere fragments that I was privy to. The rest of her lay underground, yet to be discovered, open only to her own excavations.

Occasionally, when I see the remnant of the child I remember in either of my daughters' actions, I quiver with a pang of loss, sharp and unexpected. I long to scoop that once-familiar small body into my arms. Once in a great while, I still come across a clue I haven't seen before: a rose pressed in a forgotten book, a line of poetry, a postcard written but never mailed. From this excavated artifact, I learn something new about the child my daughter was. I follow her down hallway after hallway, around every corner, crumb to crumb like Hansel and Gretel through the forest. I add this new information to my filtered memories. I shine a light on it, hold it up next to the young woman I know today, and like the rotation of a kaleidoscope, the shards drop into a slightly altered pattern.

The rose, the poem, the unmailed postcard offer incontrovertible evidence that my daughters' lives are, and always have been, their own. Even when they were young, even when their daily lives weighed so heavily on my determination to get it right, even then, they were escaping to their own fields of dreams. I turn the chipped shard over and over in my hand, in wonderment that a winged creature ever rested near. I love a mystery, I say to myself, as I tenderly replace the fragment exactly the way I found it.

Sky

I have seen spectacular displays of sky in my time. Three—okay four—stand out.

In the Ozarks in 1972, my husband and I and a bunch of friends lay on the balcony of an A-frame cabin and watched a meteor shower. Tubes of light streaking and gone, streaking and gone.

In Madrid, as we returned from a walk, the entire western sky turned blood red. We clambered up the four-foot base of a streetlamp to get a better view over the city walls.

At a Sandhills Retreat, on a moonless night, I stood on a second story deck with a group of writers, awed to silence by the inky sky pricked with myriad points of light.

During the pandemic, walking at Lakewood Cemetery in late afternoon, we witnessed a panoply of pink, overhead and left and right, a soothing blanket of sky.

Yesterday I read in the newspaper that scientists have discovered a star never before seen on the outer perimeter of our solar system. And here's the thing: that star is not there. It has taken millions of years for the light to reach Earth. The stars we see are phantoms. If that doesn't shake your confidence in your ability to perceive truth, I don't know what will.

INTERSECTIONS of
LIFE and ART

Carnal Appetites

QUICKSAND

My brother and I are too young to be at the river by ourselves. We've walked a mile through high prairie grass, carrying pitchforks to spear carp. The North Platte sprawls in this corner of Nebraska, the water widening like liquid poured in a frying pan. Rivulets trickle around islands and sandbars. The cocoa mud on the riverbank gushes between our toes. The air vibrates with insect buzz. I limp, having punctured the side of my foot with my pitchfork. We skip rocks. The sun streaks our hair. We have only one fear, and my brother voices it. "Watch out for quicksand."

Once voiced, the fear paralyzes me. I stand on the bank of the river, afraid to budge. My foot throbs. The water swirls muddy brown, hiding the bottom of the river. One false step, and I might fall through. Disappear. Ooze into oblivion.

My brother has moved out ahead of me. Running to catch up with him is how I stabbed my foot in the first place. I'm starting to wish I'd stayed home. I bite my bottom lip, willfully lift my leg, and plant it down, daring the sand to do its work.

ANIMAL RIGHTS

My mother and I served as bird dogs. We walked through dried cornfields and flushed hiding birds into the open. A pheasant would take flight, a long, low trajectory, and hazard being shot down by my father or one of my older brothers. I can conjure the taste of fall on my tongue, the rustle of cornstalks against my cheek, the sinking of boots into mud. I smell the residue of a shotgun blast, sulfurous fire and ash. I hear the slide-knock of a single action bolt. Part of me rises on the wings of the pheasant, hoping its evasive bird skills will land us both safely behind a nearby windbreak. Another part of me already savors the sweet, wild flavor of pan-fried pheasant.

Once, on the way home after a fruitless afternoon, we chanced upon two pheasants sunning on the side of the road. Mom urged my dad to stop. Dad argued that it was too near sundown, the hour when legal hunting ends. That's ridiculous, Mom countered. Ever practical, she pointed out that we'd been hunting all afternoon, and five minutes wouldn't make a bit of difference. Dad pulled the car over, unable to quell the logic of her argument. My brother propped his arm against the open doorframe and fired his shotgun. Both birds fell with one blast, and Dad flung them into the trunk. Not far down the road, we heard thumping. The back of the car rocked. Stopping again, we piled out to see what had happened. Dad eased up the trunk. Both pheasants stood on their feet staring at us. Stunned, Dad said. Then, he grabbed each pheasant by the neck and swung the bodies in circles, like a cowboy with a double lariat. Dead in his hands, dead for sure. Dad tossed their limp bodies back in the trunk.

I wished, then, he hadn't done that. I wished he would have let them go, given them a fighting chance. My father had rules about hunting that recognized the tensions inherent in taking a life to sustain life. Never shoot a sitting bird. Never shoot after sundown. Never take more than your limit. Within those rules, hunting was a contest of wit, skill, and instinct. As a non-shooting bird dog, present for the kill and later to enjoy the meat, I walked a delicate balance between dread and hunger. There was something primeval astir in the air of those autumn afternoons, and I stood before it with horror and awe. I was a novitiate confronting the mysteries. Wringing the necks of two pheasants stunned by one shot fired after sundown broke the rules, shattered the mystery, and left me sitting in the back seat of a battered Buick on a dark wad of discomfort.

By suppertime, I had all but forgotten. Mom served the pheasant pan-fried, with mashed potatoes and garden beans. She cut the large breast into several chunks so that it could be shared by a family of five. I tore the tough meat with my teeth and relished the sweet, gamy flavor. I removed an occasional piece of shot from my mouth with my fingers. I scraped the bones into the trash, rescued a long, burnished tail feather to add to my collection. By bedtime, I was as removed from the carnality of the hunting scene as I am now when I purchase meat swabbed in plastic from a local grocery.

While in England years ago, my husband and I saw enormous ring-necked pheasants roaming the hills of Yorkshire. Majestic and free, they strutted like lords of manors. Bronze and green plumage glittered against fields of yellow-blooming rapeseed. I admired their beauty and heard the distant echo of a shotgun. Flooded again with dread and hunger, I wondered how anyone could shoot them and which local pub might be serving pheasant that evening.

HUMAN RITES

I have been plagued by religion all of my life. Growing up lonely and isolated, I loved God and the prairie, and I could barely distinguish between the two. Wheat fields were God's hair undulating in the breeze. God's breath, the breeze itself, clattered the cottonwood leaves like castanets. Milkweed pods were God's breasts, goldenrod God's scepter, and needlegrass God's game of darts. God made a ladder of the hills so I could climb up, up with my eyes, lift them to the heavens, where God splayed the Milky Way with a wide paintbrush. God's eyes twinkled in the stars, and God's fingers pulled apart the knuckles of snake-grass. Dragonflies I chased up the dirt road, wild roses that pricked my fingers, cattails that exploded, white and fluffy, all spoke to me of God.

It was then, and is now, harder for me to locate God in church. Still, I try, because I long to love God in good company. I've tried so hard, in fact, that I attended seminary and got ordained. As an ordained woman, I found myself unemployed, co-opted by male clergy, and radically politicized. In my effort to belong, I had merely increased my sense of exile.

In this frame of mind, I took a trip back East to visit the sites of former Shaker colonies. I had been commissioned to write a play for the 1993 Re-Imagining Conference, an international gathering focused on feminist theologies, and I wanted to write about the Shakers. In New York, New Hampshire, and Maine, I stood on the grounds of one of the most successful communal living experiments in history. The Shakers endured for more than two hundred years and, in their heyday, boasted thousands of members. Despite their practice of celibacy, they grew in number. Misfits, spiritual seekers, runaway slaves, battered women, orphans, the homeless, jobless, sick, or poor knocked on Shaker doors and found a home. I stepped into the past at Hancock Village and heard wisps of laughter. Ghosts reached out their hands to me, beckoned me to join in spiraling circles, and I longed to slip my fingers into their palms.

As a Shaker woman, I would be allowed a position of spiritual leadership. I might become an Elder, equal to a male counterpart. I might, if I had other talents, become a Trustee and take charge of account books or the management of a line of business, the marketing of herbs or baskets or woven goods. When I prayed, I would address Mother and Father God. I might take fancy goods to market, offer laced boxes and ruffled hats to middle-class nineteenth-century women bound in corsets, bored with lives of conspicuous consumerism and barred from boardrooms and industry. I would join my sisters and brothers in worship, stomp and dance in swirling rings, sing of the gifts of simplicity. On feast days, I would rise early, play-act elaborate rituals, dress myself in imaginary robes, drink from pretend cups, sweep dust from under beds and cobwebs off windowpanes, singing "Low, low, low! I will sweep as I go, For this Mother bids me and it is my delight."

Yet, I cannot so easily slip my hand into the offered palm of once-exiled ghosts. One aspect of Shaker life confounds me. They managed all this gender equality by repressing sexuality. They denied humanness and struggled mightily to rise above it. They wanted to be angels, not mortals with flesh that hungers for the touch of flesh.

As a woman living in a sex-confused culture, I can understand the impetus behind their convictions. The history of the English founder,

Ann Lee, is the story of a woman undone by the traps of female embodiment. The uneducated daughter of a blacksmith, she married a man she did not love and dutifully bore four children, who all died in early childhood. At age thirty-four, Ann Lee was thrown into prison for disrupting the Sabbath. While in prison, she had a vision. She saw before her the perfectibility of human nature, free from the bondage of carnal appetite. She adopted this vision as her mission. She would teach a new way of life, where everyone would be equal regardless of gender, race, or age. In 1773 she led a small band to America to establish a new society based on four principles: celibacy, community, peace, and equality.

The Shakers managed their life of purity by separating men and women. Although everyone slept under the same roof, buildings had separate doors, separate stairways. Each woman was assigned one man to care for, make his bed, sew buttons on his clothing, but she was not allowed in his room until forty-five minutes after he'd left for his work of the day, so that none of his body heat would remain to tempt her. Group activities afforded little opportunity for forbidden liaisons, and members were encouraged to report suspicious flirtations to the Elders as a way of helping each other resist the lure of wanton appetite. For one hour, one day a week men and women were paired off to speak to one another, verbal intercourse, on facing chairs placed six feet apart, several pairs to a room.

Shaker life was not devoid of joy. People traveled for miles to observe their celebrative worship. Nor was their communal life lacking in love. Bonds were strong and elastic, welcoming and loyal. The Shakers simply wanted to sustain the innocence of childhood. They wanted to turn aside from the mess of living. No sex, no childbirth, no nursing, no tangle of confused relationships. Instead, everything orderly, efficient, codified, and predictable. Everyone equal, and everyone belonging.

I long for the safety of such a system. I see myself wake in the morning, slide my feet into simple slippers that carry me through a day of patterns: meals, prayers, work, and sleep. I am free from worry, my soul flies to Heaven, and no one can hurt me. Except. One morning I notice a butterfly, green and luminous silver; its wings flutter and it darts toward a pond, and I follow it. I stand transfixed while it parts the petals of a lily with its proboscis. My slippers ooze into the soft mud of the pond. The hem of my dress gets dirty. I remove my bonnet and let the breeze toss my hair. A frog sticks out its tongue to snatch a water bug. Leafy trees fill the air like a bouquet. The sun throws rays that bounce off the water, plays catch with the glistening stones, shines and shines and brushstrokes the world with blessing. I am filled with awe and hunger.

As a Shaker, I figure I would last about a day.

MUDDY WATER

Carnality does not sit easy in the human psyche. When it comes to sensual appetite, we exploit, we control, we deny, we misuse, we abuse, and, in the twenty-first century, we spend vast amounts of money on self-help books, therapy, and sexually charged entertainment. Occasionally we get it right, two bodies bump together, or a single rose moves us to ecstasy, or a painting on the wall of an art museum wrings us with dismay, and then we quiver with awareness and wonder how we blundered onto such holy ground.

The extreme edges of our discomfort are manifested by pornography, on the one hand, and spiritualization, on the other. While pornography dives into the flesh and spiritualization attempts to rise above it, both deny relationship with the body. With pornography, objectification displaces intimacy and voyeurism precludes true feeling. With spiritualization, the body is cast off from the soul entirely. It turns out that the Shakers were as indebted to a classic body/spirit dualism as any hard-core pornographer.

This conclusion bothers me a great deal. I want equality, but I don't want to dis-inhabit my body to get it. The whole muddy business makes me cringe. It's enough to make me want to root myself on the shore and never risk a single step.

We raised chickens, and the whole purpose was to kill and eat them.[1] Platters of golden fried chicken, chicken wings in barbecue sauce, roast chicken with stuffing and gravy, chicken salad, chicken chow mein, chicken soup, chicken enchiladas, livers and hearts and necks and gizzards, breasts and backs and thighs. Chicken deboned, chicken on the bone, chicken carcasses. Skinless, with skin. Fried, grilled, roasted, braised, pan-seared, stewed, boiled, and steamed. Sliced, diced, shredded, torn, pounded, tenderized, rolled, or pricked. Ripped apart with the teeth, chewed and tongued, then swallowed.

No noble hunt, here. No mystery, no reverence. I hated the chickens, especially the evil rooster who flew at me, wings pumping, beak arrowed at my eyes, until one day my father had enough and slaughtered the rooster for stew. We bought the chickens as fluffy yellow handfuls, a hundred in a low cardboard box. Sometimes we penned them in the kitchen, newspapers spread on the linoleum, the scrabble of tiny bird feet punctuating the musical cheep-cheep of baby voices. When they were old enough, we moved them to the chicken house. We fed them grain, gave them water, pampered and plumped them until they were ripe, and then we picked them.

On butchering day, the whole family got involved. Dad and Mom killed the chickens. Dad chopped their heads off, holding their necks over a bloodied stump and bringing a huge knife down with one swift swoop. Mom devised her own method. She forced the chicken's neck to the ground, placed a stick over it, stood with one foot on either end, then pulled the chicken by its legs until its head came off. Once decapitated, the bodies were flung to the ground, where headless chickens flopped and sometimes danced, bleeding into the hard-baked soil. I watched all this from a distance, chewing on the thumb of a knitted mitten. If I moved too close, the lurching headless bodies seemed to follow me like stalkers.

Dad built a big fire in the yard and set a galvanized washtub over the coals. When the water boiled, he quickly dipped each dead chicken. Steaming, the wet chickens were handed to me for picking. The large feathers came off easily, in handfuls, but the pin feathers required careful attention, each one pinched between finger and thumb like removing a thorn. The feathers stuck to my hands. I held the bloody neck stump away from me. The yellow, scaly feet poked me in the belly. The body of the chicken flopped loose. After the picking, Dad held the chickens over an open flame to singe the hair off. A flaming newspaper left black soot that had to be scrubbed off under cold well water.

I hated the smell, metallic burn and barnyard rot. Scalded chickens, wet feathers, and blood. The whole enterprise was repugnant to me but without moral implications. It was a nasty job that life required, like scrubbing down the outhouse or spreading manure on the garden.

The cleaning required more expertise. My brother, only three years older than me, was a champion with a knife. He and my mother ran races. They stood on opposite sides of a cast-off kitchen table, three naked chickens piled to their left, their shirt fronts and the table streaked with blood and random chicken bits. Each had a pail beside them on the floor for guts and feet. Mom yelled Go, and each grabbed a chicken with their left hand, a butcher knife with their right. They chopped off wings and legs, cut between the thigh and drumstick. Sliced open the body cavity, split the back and tail away from the chest to expose the guts. Yanked the guts loose, careful not to burst the green and acrid spleen. Dropped the guts in the bucket. Cut off the wishbone, split the breast, broke the ribs to remove the small, curved bones, lopped off the tail, flung the parts into another pan of water, grabbed the second chicken. All of this accompanied by competitive hoots and hollers. The year my brother turned fourteen, my mother could not out-butcher him. No matter how many chickens they lined up, five, ten, a dozen, he won. Wings, legs, backs, thighs, piled high in blue roasting pans, later to be bagged and frozen. Sometimes, in one day we slaughtered and dressed a hundred chickens.

I stood at another counter and cleaned gizzards. A chicken gizzard is roughly the size and shape of a small yo-yo. I held each hard clump in my hand, found the center seam, sliced it open, and peeled out the inner sack of gravel. Gizzard after gizzard, no competitive fuel, no one paying attention. I listened to Mom and my brother laughing, their hands flying through guts and chicken parts. We stopped raising chickens before I graduated out of picking and cleaning gizzards.

When I eventually had children, each of my daughters went through a stage of discomfort at eating identifiable body parts. Wings and legs? Backs and breasts? I sympathized with my city-bred children. In grade school, we visited a meat-packing plant, watched while cattle were electrically prodded up a narrow chute where a shirtless, bloodied man swung a huge mallet and knocked each animal dead with one well-aimed blow. We walked through rooms of hanging carcasses, blood streaming to floor drains. After viewing vats of various body parts, white chips of bone, gristly globs of fat, bits of meat, and shreds of organs, all thirteen students from my country grade school vowed we'd never eat another hot dog.

Innocence is one way of attempting to move through the vagaries of life. We can stand on the shore, refuse to budge, and hope against hope that no one confronts us with knowledge we'd rather not have. Ground meat is easier to swallow than a recognizable leg, unless, of course, you have seen the bloody slab before it enters the grinder.

Those days of barnyard carnage strike me now as a step away from innocence and into intention. When I push my hands into garden dirt every spring, I do it to jerk myself awake. Ashes make good soil for roses, and that is worth remembering.

HUMAN RITES

In the archives of a Shaker library in Maine, I found the central character for my play. I arrived at Sabbath Day Lake on a rainy day, spent and discouraged. I had missed seeing Canterbury through a fluke of scheduling, and now I learned that Sabbath Day Lake had closed for the season one day before my arrival. I walked down a narrow paved road to the cemetery. I leaned on a fence and looked into a peaceful wooded lot, the graves marked with identical cast-iron markers. Simple and uniform, the scene reminded me of rows of white gravestones I'd seen at Gettysburg or Andersonville or Arlington. I took a photograph, not knowing that a month later my house would be broken into, my camera stolen, and all the pictures from this trip lost. Even without that premonition, I was starting to doubt the sanity of this venture. What was I looking for?

I wandered back to the gift shop, where I pled my case to the attendant. I wanted permission to walk around the grounds, poke my nose inside the meeting house. She listened, thin-lipped, cotton-dressed, unmoved. Then, quietly she asked, "Would you like to see the library?"

She walked me across the road to another building and showed me into a wood-lined room filled with Shaker archives. There I spent a happy afternoon, poring over original writings and drawings. There, I came across the work of Hannah Cahoon.

Hannah's drawing of a Tree of Life, a common theme in Shaker art, did not conform to Shaker expectations. The Shakers believed their drawings were gifts from spirits who wanted to communicate with the members. Most drawings were rigidly codified and contained writings that sound like the archaic scriptural voice of some forgotten prophet. Hannah's drawing contained no writing. Rather than the typical subdued blues and whites, Hannah's work flashed with red and green. It was done in heavy opaque paint, not translucent inks and watercolors. Unlike most Shaker drawings, which are strictly symmetrical to emphasize harmony, Hannah's leaves and fruit were subtly off balance, giving her work an individual and sophisticated vision. Finally, in the bottom right-hand corner, on the front of the drawing, I spied a signature: Hannah Cahoon. Other Shaker artists did not sign their work, as that would have been a symbol of arrogance and individuality.

I fell in love with Hannah Cahoon. Like me, she must have felt both drawn to community and exiled. Like me, she might have been plagued by religion all her life, unable to forget and unable to conform. I found evidence to suggest that Hannah was not a very good Shaker. Although committed to equality, the Shakers assigned seats in worship. Scholars disagree on whether this seating denoted privilege, but apparently it held enough significance to be recorded in the archives. Hannah spent her entire adult life as a Shaker, and yet, she sat in the rear.

I took Hannah Cahoon home with me, and I lived with her through the months of writing my play. Daily we discussed the problems of raising daughters and pursuing art. We debated the relative costs of fitting in and not fitting in. I asked her if she missed sex, and she laughed. You have such a narrow view of power and pleasure, she told me. Then she spoke of work, struggling to design a collar that turns in a new way; of gathering honey from a hive, licking the sweetness off her fingers; of sitting by the cot of a dying friend, privileged to wait while she lingered on the threshold of death. Hannah talked long into the night, and she said the simplest things, and all of them seemed holy to me, and when I woke the next morning, I could remember only two words. Choose life.

BAPTISM

I'm taking Hannah with me to the river. We're standing on the bank when she lifts her foot to enter the muddy water. Wait. I grab her by the elbow. Quicksand, I say. She nods and hesitates. Our feet sink into the cocoa mud of the riverbank; soon it will slime over the tops of our toes. My brother shows up, standing on a sandbar, grinning. He's a kid again, with curly yellow hair and freckles on his nose. He's wearing rolled up jeans, an old cotton shirt, white with brown cowboy hats printed on it. For a moment, I think the sun flashes off a butcher knife, but it's only a pitchfork for spearing carp. I hear music, childlike Shaker songs that pinwheel and somersault, but underneath I feel the pulse of rhythm, dark and throbbing. I look up and down the river, wanting some assurance, a clear signal of stop or go. But there's only me and Hannah, standing with our arms entwined, hip to hip, and I feel her body heat, and we take the step, and the muddy water spreads in widening circles.

Cathedrals and Cottonwoods

On a trip to Barcelona, I stood in the sanctuary of La Sagrada Familia, Gaudi's famous yet unfinished cathedral. Head back, I lifted my eyes to soaring columns, which branched into graceful catenary arches. Gaudi took his inspiration from trees. Today, I chanced upon a bench in an old grove of cottonwoods in the Sandhills of Nebraska. Seven gnarled trunks stretched skyward toward our only hope of heaven. Leaves shimmered in a gentle canopy, the midday sun scattering the light much like Gaudi's stained-glass windows. Waxy leaves chattered on the breeze. Breathless and awestruck in both cathedrals, I tasted transcendence. Yet one was orderly, artful, harnessed to perfection, a step toward eternity; the other wild, aged, flawed, smacking of eventual decay. This is the primeval tension, isn't it? Confronted with beauty, we strive to bottle it for safekeeping, but it is rendered more precious by the ephemeral. Robert Frost said it best: "Nothing gold can stay."

I am of an age where illness and death occur with regularity. I am, today, on a writer's retreat. There are seven of us: two have lost spouses to cancer, I have survived a cancer diagnosis, another has a schizophrenic daughter, one's wife struggles with cranial nerve shingles. My husband's friend and former boss, seventy-five years old, went to sleep on a Friday night and did not wake up Saturday morning. Does this make us despair and go screaming into the night? Occasionally, but mostly no. Instead, most of us are tenderized, cognizant of fleeting time, sensitized to graceful encounters, open to hope. I was deeply moved and inspired by Gaudi's cathedral, but I felt understood by the gnarled and struggling cottonwoods.

I wonder about all this as an artist. Some of us—writers, painters, sculptors, architects—strive to create work that will speak to succeeding generations. Picasso's Guernica. Shakespeare's everything. Frank Gehry's Guggenheim. Most, like me, grasp a moment, offer it to the world, and if we're lucky, it is held momentarily, like a bouquet of cut flowers, before it is forgotten or relegated to the trash. But some artists create the ephemeral on purpose. There is a man in Minnesota named Peter Juhl who builds sculptures of balanced rocks, subject to changing weather, shifting winds, even passersby. He knows his sculptures won't last; that is the point. He captures them in photographs, but the photos are no substitute for the real-world sight of rocks defying gravity. Right now, at the Minnesota Landscape Arboretum, there stands a willow castle named YouBetcha, complete with a moat and five turrets, that will reign for a life cycle before the elements return it to the soil. The artist, Patrick Dougherty, has built Stickwork all over the world and earned numerous awards, but the work itself is temporary. The honesty of this art speaks to me. These defiant artists accept, even celebrate, the impermanence of our existence.

About those cottonwoods. Situated on a sloping marsh, the floor had many times shifted. The bases of the trees were a labyrinth of ropy roots, searching for a firm foundation. On a drive around Lake Superior, I witnessed a tree growing straight up from a rock, its roots suspended through air to soil four or five feet across a ravine. Everything wants to live.

One day the cottonwoods will lose their struggle to find a footing. On a remote island in Rainy Lake in northern Minnesota, I have seen twenty-foot pines knocked down by a wayward wind, their roots pulled away from the rock where they've perched for decades. Gaudi's cathedral may last for generations, but it, too, is vulnerable to fire, natural disasters, or the threats of modern terrorism and war.

I drive regularly past a lovely cemetery in Minneapolis. All who lie there are dead. Everyone struggles to live, and yet no one survives being mortal. I find this combination of struggle and decay beautiful and soothing. I love my backyard garden most in the fall, when the hostas and sedum are wild and spent, preparing for the mock death of winter. The maple trees flame out in glory before standing as magnificent skeletons. The begonias and snapdragons push their energy through green fuses to produce seed, one last hurrah before joining a throng of annuals in the compost bin. Within this spectacle are dual promises: life, in some form, goes on, and the dead feed the living.

Sitting among the old-growth cottonwoods, I note the deep vertical ridges of the bark, furrowed with age like cheeks of old women whose lives are spent toiling in the sun. I place my whole hand within the crease of one sister tree. She holds me, and we are one.

Egg Carton Art

Why don't you just hire it done, she says to me, and I wonder what planet she grew up on, this friend of mine, who can't buy a painting for her home without first checking with her decorator. Poor child, I think, who never turned macaroni into art, glued paper cones onto window screen, laid out elbow, shell, and bowtie in muffin tins, traced ornate symmetrical designs, spray painted the whole thing gold and stood back filled with pride and awe. No tall juice cans drilled with holes, laced with twine, worn like shoes or stilts or braces, arms stiff to work Pinocchio feet. No listening to the scrunchy suck of cans to dirt, round tracks heralding the coming or the going, the coming or the going of God knows what.

Why, I know a guy who holds his sewage system together with nothing but wire and white paste. My dad invented a gadget to slice corn off the cob lickety-split. Once, when his Parkinson's fingers shook too much to remove his new shirt, he cut the buttons off with a nail clipper. Didn't want to wrinkle it, he said. We fixed our bathroom stool with a wad of chewing gum. Temporary, but still.

Sing praises, sing praises, that's what I think, gazing at a dressing table covered in seashells, a white lace tablecloth thumbtacked to the rounded rim, the head of Marilyn Monroe rising from it as if the curves of the table itself constitute a billowing bosom. Once, at the Minnesota State Fair, I saw a suit of armor made of coveralls covered in duct tape. Bottle cap art was big when I was a kid and long chains of chewing gum wrappers. My kids threaded beads onto safety pins, replaced the laces in their sneakers. My family once paid a lot of money to ship home a painted rock from Truchas, New Mexico. We chose it from a garden of painted rocks, mute and costumed on a drop of white, fresh-fallen snow. The painting is either three women and a shoe or a bright green fish, who can tell, and who, other than my expert-seeking friend, could care?

I've seen a man made from a rusty muffler. There's no end to what you can do with peacock feathers. My old piano teacher once sewed me a yellow gathered skirt, layer after layer of rickrack, and around the waistband, a million, maybe two, gold baby safety pins, row on row of click and clatter. I started a trend in high school wearing a shellacked chicken bone on a chain as a necklace. Later, I found a diaper pin in the gutter and pinned it to my letter jacket as a good luck charm.

In the panhandle of Nebraska, somebody recreated Stonehenge out of old junk cars. Gray cars, precariously perched, stacked and balanced, measuring the rise and fall of the sun, marrying pop culture and the sublime. They named it Carhenge, and nobody knows if it is a joke or art. Nothing is merely what it seems. Everything can be twisted and dropped on its head, another turn of the kaleidoscope, and nothing in the Guggenheim or the Tate or the National Art Gallery restores my hope like looking at tulips cut from egg cartons.

God Is Not a TV Repairman

In my hometown, nestled in the heart of the North Platte River Valley in the western panhandle of Nebraska, there was a TV and radio repairman named Gene. Gene was a local legend, a wizard with electronics, but decidedly short on interpersonal skills. He lived alone. He didn't answer his telephone. He had a message machine, but he didn't return calls. If you had work for him, you'd call the local Gambles store and leave a message. Anytime Gene's name came up, whether in the Jack and Jill grocery, in the Prairie Winds community center, or in the foyer of the First Baptist Church, someone would inevitably say, "That Gene, he's a genius. He can fix anything . . . if you can get him."

Lest you think I exaggerate, let me tell you that in 1982 my mother called Gene to look at her ailing TV. Gene said it needed a tube he had to order, and he'd get back to her. A month or so later Mom married a man who moved in with her and brought a TV. Thinking they'd keep Mom's now tubeless TV as a backup, they pushed it into a corner of the bedroom and waited. Months went by, a year, then five years, then ten. Occasionally Mom would pass Gene on the street, he'd hold up a finger and say, "Marge, I haven't forgot about that tube."

Fifteen years later, long after my stepfather had died, Gene still hadn't shown up with the missing tube. I was visiting my mother in November, the week before an anticipated sacred event, a televised Nebraska football game, when her second TV went on the fritz. She frantically tried to get hold of Gene: called his house, called the Gambles store. Miraculously, he returned her call and promised to come the next day. We stayed home waiting all day: twenty-three games of Scrabble, 102 games of cribbage, no Gene. In her frustration, Mom told all her friends and anyone else who would listen. They all shook

their heads and said, "That Gene, he's a genius . . . if you can get him."
My cousin Paul stopped by and told us that the last time he needed
Gene, he found out where he was working, drove there, and refused
to leave until Gene got in the pickup with him. "That Gene," Paul said.
"He can fix anything . . . if you can get him." Not able to see ourselves
either stalking or kidnapping, Mom and I waited. And waited.

Early, very early, Saturday morning—the very day of the football
game—the front doorbell rang. In my flannel nightshirt, I yelled at
Mom in the back bedroom. She was on the phone with a friend. We
did a bit of frantic pantomiming—you go, you go, I'm not dressed,
hurry up, I don't have a robe, he'll leave—and that's how I found
myself running my hands through my bed head and grinning around
the edge of the door at the local genius TV repairman. Mom and I
were giddy with the taste of freedom after three days housebound
and waiting when, maybe thirty minutes later, Gene informed us that
he had to leave to go get a part. We looked at each other aghast. We
couldn't let him out the door; we knew we'd never see him again. As
if reading our minds, Gene offered to leave his tools for collateral.
Reluctantly Mom and I watched him depart and settled into another
day of waiting. After several hours, he did come back, he worked his
magic, and we had television, in the nick of time for opening kickoff.
While writing the check, Mom asked Gene about the TV in the corner
of her bedroom, the one she'd been hoarding for fifteen years. Gene
said two things. 1) He had that part, but he forgot to bring it; and 2)
That TV wasn't worth fixing anyway, never was worth much.

Now, all these years later, the thing that strikes me about Gene, the
illusory genius who could—if he would only show up—fix anything,
is that this is how I, too often, relate to God. As if God could fix
anything if He (or She, but when I'm thinking like this, it's usually
He) would just show up. So, I wait. And plead. And I fidget. And I
think of ways to trick Him. I'd stalk Him if I knew how. I court His
favor—anything so He'll come by and fix things. Like that famous

and heartbreaking Beckett play, I wait and wait and wait for Godot, and Godot never comes.

Of course not. Because God is not a TV repairman.

I know better. I have years of education in theology and spiritual thought. Whatever you or I call that nebulous sense of spiritual power adrift in the universe and laying claim to our imaginations, we should know by now we can't use our gods to get what we want.

There are lots of different gods. And maybe you're not even waiting for something you think of as god. Maybe you're waiting for a stroke of luck. Or the right partner. Or a better job. Something only you can name that will make things all better. Casting your lot with magical thinking, gritting your teeth through pain and loss, holding yourself in abeyance until the worst is over. Only, when is it ever over?

Do you know that famous Henry James short story "The Beast in the Jungle"? A man believes he's destined for something momentous, even terrible, and he waits for it. He meets a woman who loves him, but he cannot give himself to love because he's waiting for this beast to arrive. The woman dies. He's grieving in the churchyard when the realization hits him that his fate has met him with a vengeance, for while waiting, he has refused to live. He has become the man to whom nothing on earth has happened. He could have escaped this wretched fate if he had loved her, but in his egoism, he missed his chance.

Today I went for a walk. Damp, cold, and dreary, as is typical of Minnesota in March. I decided not to wait for a better day. I walked out, and I saw things: greening pachysandra, the creek near my house running free of ice, a soaring hawk. A gray-bearded man passed me on a curved footbridge and smiled. I stepped over chalk drawings on the sidewalk. Patches of blue in the somber sky. Trees budding. It was enough—just enough—to make a person's heart sing.

Because the Poet Died

I did not grow up wanting to write. I did write, but I wrote for fun. Or because I loved words and language and books, and writing was a way to explore that world. But I never thought of myself as a writer.

For one thing, I come from a rural Nebraska community, and never once, in all the years of my childhood, did I meet a working writer. I went to the library for books, and I went to the movies to see films. Both seemed to me like gifts from the gods, dropped into my ordinary life from some other plane of existence.

For another thing, my brothers and I were conditioned to be practical. My father, who knew only farming, sold all his farm machinery and tried to make it as a songwriter. Complicating his status as a dreamer was the harsher reality of failing health, so by the time I was nine, my mother was the primary wage earner. My mother, whose natural gifts were a quick mind, boundless energy, and courage, grew suspicious of anything that would not lead directly to a good job. She wanted all her children to be free from the constraints of poverty. Reading was a luxury, even a waste of time. The world of art was a fantasy that ordinary people could not afford.

A third thing was that I read too many fairy tales. I thought that if you had artistic talent, you would be discovered. Someone would notice. When I went to college and majored in English (with the practical plan of teaching), I avoided creative writing courses. If I had any talent, I reasoned, I'd know it by now. I had a friend who was a poet, and I envied her, but that was as close as I got.

A few years shy of thirty, I met a woman who believed she could write. To my surprise, Ruth was an ordinary mortal. Since we had a lot in common—married, small children, readers—I thought, if Ruth can do it, I can do it.

I started by writing poetry. Because poems are short. A few words on a page seemed possible. I wrote the kinds of poems I had studied in college. I wrote sonnets and rhyming couplets and quatrains. I struggled with meter and rhyme, labored over word choice, pushed my daily life through the sieve of language, groped with webbed fingers for intricate possibilities. I sat up late at night, stretched my children's nap time, carried a pencil and pad with me to waiting rooms. I wrote about my children, the thrill of an organ concert, and my disappointment when betrayed by a friend.

By the time Ruth and I packed ourselves, without children or husbands, off to a writer's conference, I couldn't wait to meet with the poet-teacher who would be attending. I knew I had hard work to do, but I was confident that he would identify a spark in me. I was eager to be inspired, to be guided, because by then I'd figured out a secret: writing can be learned. The requisite qualification is less about talent than desire. The gift is not what you possess; the gift is what writing brings to your life, and you have to want it badly enough to persevere and put up with criticism. In my youthful vigor and naive love, I set out with high hopes.

The poet didn't show up for the conference. He'd had a heart attack the night before and died. The man assigned to deal with aspiring poets was a writer of self-help books. Twenty-three of them.

I met with Him the first afternoon of the conference. He was big and full-bearded, and He sported a hearty laugh. He wore glasses, corduroys, and a chambray shirt open at the throat. He suggested we sit in a cozy window seat on the stairway landing of the writer's lodge. Though the lodge was a majestic old building with many available rooms, this spot overlooked the lake, picturesque, private, and small. With the glow of the afternoon sun spilling over my precious pages, He told me my poems were terrible.

"What's this about?" He said of the poem I had written about my daughter. "Why should we care about this?" He asked of another. The sonnet that had held me attentive through several afternoons fell to the floor. "Old fashioned," He said. "There's no life here. Nothing to grab hold of. Do it like this." He handed me a poem by a colleague of His that was, I think, about ants progressing through the hierarchy of an anthill. It was, no doubt, deep and metaphorical, but I was too wounded to care. He placed His hand on my knee, leaned in, and said, "I can help you. In private sessions."

I fled. I knew I could not sit with Him, either in private sessions or in class. I later learned that He had a notorious reputation as a womanizer. The odd thing, as I look back on this, is that even though I knew His hand on my knee was creepy, I never doubted His pronouncements about my work. A working writer will think me too fragile, unable to take criticism. But the point is, I wasn't a working writer. I was a lover of writing, and there is a difference. And since I had found out, on the first day of a week-long conference, that I was a mere impostor and not a poet at all, I had a problem.

I solved my dilemma that week by wandering into the friendliest class I could find. I heard laughter and stood in the doorway until bid to enter. The teacher, a dark-haired, vibrant woman with an East Coast accent, wrote short dramatic pieces to augment church services. I listened to her, read her examples, and said to myself, I can do that. And I did.

Short dramas for a youth group my husband and I led, then six produced plays, a few years as co-director of a small theater company, a number of small performance pieces, a lengthy professional foray into theological exploration, and then four published books of fiction. All this because the poet died.

It might have gone differently. Perhaps, the poet does not have a heart attack and arrives hale and hearty. I don't remember the poet's name, so I can't conjure the actual person, but let's say he's small, wiry, amiable. He, too, sits with me over my poems. Yes, they are stilted (though he's careful not to use that language), but he sees me for what I am, a lover of words. A student, open to learning. He encourages me. He gives me a couple prompts that turn into rich metaphors. I spend the week in an artistic haze, dazzled by possibility. I go home and write furiously. I publish five poems, in as many years, in little-known journals. Eventually, a chapbook. I write poetry, happily, for four decades, and the writing teaches me to be a keen observer, a compassionate traveler, and I feel I owe it all to this poet whose name I will never forget.

Or, I go home, write furiously, have five poems published, in as many years, in little-known journals. I grow discouraged and stop writing. I go to work for a publishing house where I spend my days reading other people's manuscripts.

Or, after publishing five poems, I decide to try writing fiction. Or I meet my eventual theater partner at a small party. She says she's interested in new work, and I decide—based on my confidence from having written five published poems—that I will attempt to write a play.

Or, after meeting with the womanizing author of self-help books, I decide the entire writing world is made up of frauds and exploiters and vow to never pick up a pencil again.

It could have gone so many ways. A life consists of some mysterious amalgam of context, serendipity, personal choice, and a host of small, seemingly insignificant-at-the-time moments.

Still, I take comfort. If our lives boil down, eventually, to a constellation of small, seemingly random moments, then every moment matters. The ripple effect of the beating butterfly's wing.

When I wandered into fiction, finally, I started by writing short stories. Because—well, yes—they are short. But mostly because short stories are predicated on small moments when a life may be slightly altered, some insight gained that will make a difference. The kind of moments that are recognized only in retrospect. Get conscious, a story says. Notice your life. That is the path to deeper meaning. And that is the truest thing I know.

Privilege

I am being interviewed for acceptance to an MFA program in creative writing. I've waited a long time for this, since I have a family and have done one or two other things before admitting that I'd much rather write. The man interviewing me is a well-respected teacher and published author, is slightly balding, wears glasses, has a cool demeanor, and doesn't look at me when he speaks. He says my writing sample, which he hasn't had time to read, shows promise. He flips through the pages, my statement of goals, my resume, my life. Then, he leans back and presses his fingertips together. "How are you going to react if someone in one of your classes questions their religious upbringing?"

"Excuse me," I say, bewildered but getting a bad feeling.

"In a graduate writing program," he goes on, his voice growing bigger, "people need to feel free to write what they think. They need to be able to question. Some people might use vulgarity or profanity. How are you going to respond to that?"

Possible responses to his question float through my head. Profanity, for starters. Or pointing out that religious discrimination is against the law. I toy, momentarily, with the direct approach: You don't know anything about me. What kind of writer are you, to be so narrow-minded and prejudicial?

"I'll be fine," I manage to say. I smile. I hate myself for groveling.

He lectures me then. Something about freedom in the classroom, a fundamentalist Christian he once knew who got upset by people's expressions. He rounds it off by saying he is only trying to protect me.

I don't know if I will be admitted. After this, I don't know if I want to be.[1]

This man based his remarks to me on information that he saw on my resume, that I have attended seminary and am an ordained member of American Baptist Churches, U.S.A. He didn't know much about Baptists, especially American Baptists, and he didn't know a thing about my personal beliefs or evolving understandings. Nor did he bother to find out. He assumed.

I was angry. I felt demeaned. Powerless and afraid. I groveled because he held the pen in his hand that could determine my immediate future.

I had not thought of this scene in years. I ran across it in my notes while working on these essays. I live in Minneapolis, the city where George Floyd was murdered. I am learning about measures my city and many other cities have taken, historically and presently, to limit opportunities for BIPOC members of our communities: racial housing covenants, red-lining, inequities in schools, voter suppression, not to mention our history of enslavement and theft of indigenous land. The list is long and heartbreaking. I am a white, well-educated, upper-middle-class woman. Excepting occasions where I've felt discriminated against for being a woman, I've enjoyed enormous privileges that I have taken for granted. I have made assumptions about people based on skin color, economics, education, and yes, even religion. I have biases predicated on what part of the country people live in. I've been blind to my prejudices, thinking I was compassionate and understanding about the way things are.

Maya Angelou wrote, "Do the best you can until you know better. Then when you know better, do better."

I am trying to do better.

So, I forgive my interviewer. I admit, painfully, that I am just like him. I apologize for my lingering righteous indignation over a brief encounter when others live with discrimination every waking moment. I am also trying to forgive myself. I hope I can do better. I hope we can all do better. And be better. Ah, humanity! I hope.

I Say Unicorns Are Real

My grandson, at age six, asked how many reindeer drive Santa's sleigh. It was Christmas Eve, and he wanted to leave carrots for the reindeer and cookies for Santa.

I counted on my fingers—Dasher, Dancer, Prancer, etc.—then concluded, "Eight, and one for Rudolph. Nine, in all."

He looked at me ever so kindly. "Oh Grandma, I don't think Rudolph is real, do you?"

Struggling not to laugh, I said, "I don't know. But we could leave nine carrots just in case. If Rudolph doesn't show up, then Santa can have it."

He agreed, but I could see he wasn't convinced. Later, snuggled together under a blue blanket in the same room with the tray of cookies and carrots, I prepared to tell this adorable blond-headed boy a story. Quickly, and with an impish grin, he snatched up the ninth carrot and ate it.

This scene reminded me of when we took two other grandchildren to see a live performance of *Rudolph, the Reindeer* at a local children's theater. Another grandson, age four, had by then seen multiple cartoon renditions of Santa Claus and his entourage. When the actors came on stage wearing headdresses with deer antlers, he leaned over and whispered to me, "But they're not real." To him, the cartoon renditions were real, but the humans wearing costumes? Highly suspect.

As adults, we go to great lengths to encourage the imaginary worlds of our children. We speak directly to their stuffed animals, allow imaginary friends a place setting at the table. I have a friend whose father was so invested in prolonging the myth of Santa Claus that he would climb out on a snow-covered roof with skis to leave sled tracks.

Yet, there comes a time—undefined and sacrosanct—when we expect children to know the difference between what is real and what is not. We label adult beliefs in the imaginary as delusionary, mental illness.

When a friend I will call Ann was suffering from age-related dementia, I visited her in a nursing facility. We conversed as usual, though I noticed that the television was on. As we prepared to go out for lunch, Ann moved over to a chair positioned in front of the television to say goodbye to a framed picture of Jesus. "Don't be frightened," Ann said to the photo. "We'll be back soon."

After lunch and on returning to her room, Ann wanted to introduce me to her friend Jesus in the picture frame. Then, seated at her table, she asked me if I thought she was crazy. "I know he's not real," she said. "But he's real to me."

Perhaps the lines between the real and the imagined are not as distinct as we like to think. Years ago, when my cousin was dying of cancer, my mother and I flew from separate places to meet at my aunt's house in Sacramento to console the grieving family. My aunt, who had already lost one adult child to a medical complication and was poised to lose another, had little faith in Western medicine. She did, however, put a lot of stock in herbal supplements. My aunt and my mother were both in the early diagnostic stages of macular degeneration, and my aunt showed us a sealed box of herbs she had purchased. She had paid a considerable sum for the box.

"Do you mix them with tea or what?" my mother asked.

"No, you just shake the box," my aunt said.

Later, Mom met me in the kitchen. "How can she believe that box of herbs is going to help her?" My mother was aghast, but she loved this dear sister and did not want to upset her.

Meanwhile, my mother, who believed in a literal Heaven, made several statements referring to my cousin's impending death and the promised reunion of loved ones in Heaven that were upsetting to my aunt. When my aunt walked out of the conversation one evening, my mother, bewildered, said, "I find it comforting to think of Heaven."

My uncle, the father of the dying daughter, said, with great kindness, "Yes, it would be, if you could believe it."

Years ago, I read a slim book that changed my understanding of how we make sense of things. Peter Berger's *A Sacred Canopy*, a sociological study of the role of religion, made a big impact on me. I am crudely paraphrasing here, but Berger argues that out of our authentic experience of mystery and spirit, we attempt an articulation, largely through metaphor. Our articulations are necessarily partial. Furthermore, we humans tend to construct a religious system that validates whatever social order we perceive as necessary for survival at the time. Therefore, you might think that religions and secular belief systems would be highly changeable, adapting as circumstances change. Instead, they tend to become institutionalized. We forget that the systems were constructs and imbue them with the power of *what is*.

I cannot resist mentioning a theater director I once knew who would say, "It's not my opinion; it's a fact." If we are honest, most of us operate that way in one sphere or another.

We all choose to believe in a reality that cannot be proven. One person's box of herbs is another person's Heaven.

A few years ago my husband and I had the good fortune of being in Oaxaca, Mexico, for the Day of the Dead celebration. We went on a day tour with a microlending organization, En Via, that took us to the pueblo of San Miguel, where we were privileged to learn about one family's traditions. We visited the cemetery, lavishly decorated with marigolds and crimson coxcomb, baskets of fruit, bottles of beer or Coca-Cola, family photos and other mementos. The decorated graves and the elaborate home altars that Oaxacans construct are meant to lure the spirits of loved ones home for twenty-four hours. When Oaxacans speak of the traditions they uphold, they use language that suggests they are willfully participating in the not-real.[1] "It is said that the saints return for twenty-four hours," they will say.

That qualifying *it is said* spoke to me of wisdom. It both keeps the knowledge that our beliefs are human constructs in the forefront of our minds and leaves room for other interpretations. How much more generous and open this attitude than our tendency to pronounce that our unproven beliefs are the way things are.

When Ann asked me if I thought she was crazy for adopting a framed picture of Jesus as her friend, I gulped for one second. It was odd. Weird, even. But crazy? Instead, isn't our adoption of the imaginary, whether religious beliefs or imaginary friends, a creative way to combat loneliness and isolation? I do not wish to diminish the too real suffering of those who hear punitive voices and cannot silence them or have other manifestations of mental disturbance that cause suffering. I do wish to say that the line between the real and the imagined is, at best, a dotted line, and it might serve the human community better if we could remember that.

My nine-year-old granddaughter recently wrote a poem. It contained this line: "I say unicorns are real." I felt a slight pang when I read that line, surely a child's defiant declaration in the face of encroaching knowledge. Or perhaps, it's her way of saying, I am willfully participating in this not-real construct. Either way, the unicorn remains a symbol of flight and freedom, beauty on the wing, and that is what matters. And that is what I told Ann about her friend Jesus in the picture frame.

Souls at White Heat

Writers have a lot in common with ancient alchemists. Alchemists, those medieval amalgams of chemists and philosophers, were interested in transformation. They wanted to turn ordinary metals into something precious. They were after gold, the philosopher's stone, but it represented more than material wealth to them. Gold also signified the elixir of life, the secrets of immortality, the stuff that makes getting out of bed seem worthwhile.

As writers, we are after transformation. We dig with ordinary tools to excavate the surprising and mysterious. While material wealth might be a nice by-product, most of us are resigned to the benefits reaped from the process itself: if not the key to the answers of life, at least an honest effort to articulate the important questions.

There are three stages to the alchemical process: putrefaction, distillation, transformation. First, you break down the existing system. Then, with everything out of balance, you apply a clarifying flame and burn off the nonessentials. Finally, with the identification of a core, transformation becomes possible.

When I began a graduate creative writing program, I found myself swimming in the putrefaction phase. I thought I knew something about writing before I got there. After all, I'd written five plays that had been on the stage. I'd published an article here and there. I'd co-edited a book that was on local library shelves. I had even taken a year off to write a bad novel that was tucked in the back of my third file drawer. I framed a quote by Virginia Woolf that said, in effect, anybody can write a mediocre novel, but it takes talent to write a truly bad one. Despite all that background, I found myself deluged with new ideas. Instead of reading to find out how to live, I was learning to read to discover how to write. My intuition, which I had counted on before, took a leave of absence. I was drowning in possibilities, chaos, and confusion.

I set out to write my first short story. Being in the putrefaction stage, I had no idea how to distill the essential elements. Somewhere in my past, I must have heard that you need to know the basics before you can depart from them, so I followed a traditional structure. I developed the story within a linear frame. I pushed toward a climactic event. I worked to illumine a major change in my main character. At the same time, I experimented with what I thought was a complex layering of a clear conflict.

Readers couldn't identify the conflict. Most thought I had four, maybe five separate stories crammed into one. Their advice: Choose one and focus.

In the same story, I purposely left out an event. I thought I was carefully selecting the critical moments on either side of a gap that added mystery and drama.

To the opening question, Did anything bother you about this story, my readers responded unanimously: You left out the critical scene. A few thought I'd inadvertently omitted a page. Their advice: If you set up a climax, don't leave it out of the story.

I wrote my story in first person because I could hear the opening sentence in the voice of the narrator: That same winter, my African violets died. I worked hard to make my narrator humanly flawed. There were scenes with her ex husband, and I did not want him to look like a simplistic jerk. I made my narrator understanding of his problems. I thought I was adding complexity.

Readers thought she was too self-aware. Their advice: Try making her less honest. Or: Try writing the story in limited third-person, so we can see her from another perspective.

Having been cautioned about writing autobiographically, I chose to write about a fictitious person. I made up the events of the story that I thought carried the most punch. When I fleshed out her character, a few emotional elements from my own life sneaked in. My narrator was struggling with the empty nest and grieving separation from her children. Not wanting to fall into a cliche, I included her grief only as a small humanizing detail.

Readers thought this was the most compelling part of the story. Their advice: Think about expanding the mother theme.

In short, I made a lot of mistakes. Feeling overwhelmed with the possibilities of choice, I stabbed in the dark. The most promising elements of the story, for my readers, were things that sneaked in alongside my purposes. The things I deliberately set out to accomplish failed or were sabotaged by other unconscious choices. What does this mean? How do we ever move through this stage of putrefaction and begin to distill the essential elements?

Crafting a story is complex and delicate work. Mistakes are part of the picture. Yet, this putrefaction stage is painful. Not the criticism, because that's helpful. Not the thought of more work. The pain springs from the fear that digging deeper will reveal nothing.

Here's a sobering truth. Whether I am a new student in a writing program or a seasoned writer, every new work is a step into the putrefaction stage. There is no creativity without this part of the process. The alchemists would argue there is no life without risking the chaos.

Emily Dickinson surely knew something about this process when she wrote, "Dare you see a Soul at the White Heat?" Words like "hammer" and "blaze" suggest that the passage through putrefaction is anything but kind and gentle. "Crouch within the door," she says, and this is what I find I must do. After mourning the failure of my first short story, I decided to let it go. I slowly opened the door of the blast furnace. I slipped inside and crouched in the corner, and I held all to the flames. I watched the fire curl the edges, lick the words off the page. Then, from among the embers, I lifted out a few glowing coals. And I started over.

Fatigue

Before I started my chemotherapy program, I called my brother and told him what everyone else had told me; the main side effect is fatigue. "Oh," he chuckled, "so, what? You'll have to take a nap every day?" We laughed, thinking that sounded like a nice respite and certainly nothing to fear.

One of my doctors did say chemo fatigue is not like other kinds of tired. She tried to warn me, but having nothing to relate to, I couldn't imagine what she meant. Relieved that the severe nausea people used to experience is controlled, for most, with drugs, I thought, Fatigue. I can handle that.

It's difficult to describe chemo fatigue. Here's what it's not: It's not, I think I'll take a nap tired. It's not, can't keep my eyes open during the 10:00 news tired. It's not even new mother up with crying baby tired. It's not the tired I felt when, only months before my diagnosis, I hiked in and out of the Grand Canyon. It's not jet lag. Body fatigue and sleep deprivation are the kinds of tired that long for rest. Just lay my head down and let me sleep tired.

Chemo tired is a different brand of tired. Chemo tired is sick and tired. In the words of the spiritual "Precious Lord," chemo tired renders you tired, weak, and worn. A restless tired. Bored out of your mind tired. Too tired to sleep. Too weak to converse. Too worn to even daydream. A profound failure of the imagination.

In the middle of my chemo rotation, I called a friend and asked her to go to an afternoon movie. I thought it would be good for me to get out of the house. We went to the Riverview, a vintage art deco movie house that I love because it's not in a strip mall, the seats are cheap, and the interior hasn't been carved up into little boxes. Plus, you can afford the popcorn. Never mind that the floor might be sticky with spilled soda or the seats creaky or the hinges broken. What I'd never noticed before was that there are no headrests on the seats. Before the movie was half over, I was so preoccupied with the effort to hold up my head that I couldn't follow the plot. I didn't care whether Jay Gatsby died in that swimming pool. All I could think about was the relief of getting home and lying flat. That's chemo tired.

Chemo works by destroying the rapidly producing cells within the body: cancer cells, hair cells, and blood cells. The cancer you can do without. Though it's disconcerting to slowly lose not only the hair on your head but eyebrows, eyelashes, facial fuzz, and pubic hair, you can do without it. Blood cells, on the other hand, you cannot live without. The trick is to dose you with enough chemical poison to permanently kill the cancer without killing all your blood cells. Red blood cells carry oxygen, and when they are depleted, you get tired.

You're supposed to drink half your body weight in fluid ounces every day. For me, that was sixty-five ounces. The purpose is to flush the chemo from your system. Too few fluids, the chemo hangs around too long, damaging the kidneys and bladder. During the last two rounds of chemo, I went to the hospital for extra IV fluids. I couldn't drink enough. Too tired.

If roadkill could get up and move, that might be chemo tired.

I had dolls in my childhood with open/shut eyes. Sometimes the eyes stuck open, dooming Betty or Kathy or Baby Tears to perpetual wakefulness. In my eight-year-old mind, I crooned lullabies, imagining my poor dollies to be eternally tired. Something like that could be chemo tired.

An unnatural tired. Chemically induced tired. Something the body doesn't recognize and therefore doesn't know how to respond to tired. Go away and leave me alone, old dog under the steps tired. Would give up if I could give up tired. A willow tree weeping, weeping, weeping kind of tired.

When somebody you love is undergoing chemo, and you ask how it's going, and they say, Okay, just a little tired, they mean chemo tired. That's all I'm saying.

A Flying Leap

"I'm getting married, and there's nothing you can do about it."

Not a phrase you want to hear from your underage daughter or son, but this was my ninety-six-year-old mother on the phone. I knew that she had a new friend, we'll call him George. He had been serving as a volunteer chaplain at Mom's assisted living residence. But a wedding? At her age! What could they be thinking?

Mom made the move to assisted living at age ninety-two, leaving the small town she'd lived in all her life to be near my older brother and his family in Fort Collins. She liked living communally, joined in every activity as if she were a kid at summer camp, and cultivated a reputation as a warm and friendly person. She became the official volunteer greeter for new residents within weeks of moving in. She financed the move with a long-term care policy that was purchased before all the current qualifiers attached to such policies. She had a pacemaker and took a fistful of medications daily, but her overall health was good. The main factor that drove her out of her home was progressive macular degeneration.

When her policy was set to run out after four years, my two older brothers and I tried to convince her to stay where she was. She had savings to finance three more years and we all offered to chip in when needed, but she wouldn't hear of it. She wanted to move to a facility that would accept Medicaid patients when the time came. She reasoned that she could still make new friends, but she might not be able to later. Living on a meager income most of her life, my mother was a genius at saving and stretching every dollar. She was not about to forfeit her independence at the end of her life.

The second assisted living facility was not a success for her. Many of the residents were in poorer health. The main activity seemed to be watching movies, which Mom could not see or had no interest in. She loved games of all kinds, but she could not find other residents either willing to join her or capable of playing.

George was a chaplain who held a service in the community room once a week. His wife had recently died after a long decline from Alzheimer's. He had started visiting my mother in her room. I knew he was special to her, and I was glad for his attentions.

But a wedding!

She sounded desperate on the phone. Only later did I learn that she had called my brothers first, in our natural birth order, and they had both been shocked and expressed reservations. My mother did not have enough assets to attract a charlatan, but none of us knew George. One brother insisted on a background check. The other said, "Why don't you just live together, if that's what you want." By the time she got to me, her defenses were entrenched.

She calmed down enough to tell me what had happened. Some residents had noticed George's special attentions to Mom and complained to the staff. The administrator walked into Mom's room unannounced, caught Mom and George embracing, and walked out. On George's way out of the building, he was summoned into the administrator's office and reminded that he was not allowed to fraternize with residents. He would no longer be able to serve as a volunteer chaplain, but he could still see Mom. The official word: fired for ethical reasons.

My mother could not comprehend why their relationship should be off limits. George, who had spent most of his ministerial life as a foreign missionary, seemed not to understand either, though it's hard for me to believe he would not have known this rule. Either way, they were busted. Embarrassed, George announced that he could no longer come see Mom. She was devastated, angry, and befuddled, and when he got down on his knees and proposed to her, she said yes. She couldn't imagine life without him.

I knew George had only a small pension. "Mom, what will you live on?"

"We'll live on love."

"You can't cook anymore. George exists on TV dinners. You said yourself he has never used his stove."

She chuckled. "I'm not going to listen to you," she said. "I've made up my mind."

Then, the final blow: "George prayed about it. God is leading this, and therefore God will provide."

I wondered where my practical mother had gone, and who was this woman impersonating her?

I struggled with a cornucopia of conflicted feelings. Had George intentionally misled my mother with his statement that he could not come see her? Was he trustworthy? Why such a rush? What if she got sick? Or he did? There were everyday considerations they paid no attention to. On the other hand, how lovely to find love so late. So what if they had only a few months together? Would he abandon her? What terrible thing could happen? That they'd live in squalor and be miserable? But wasn't she already miserable?

Eventually I wearied of her long litany of love and wonder and why have so many fallen in love with me (her third marriage) and I don't care what you think. I needed time and space to wrestle my heaving emotions to the ground. I said several times, I'm going to go. She said, "You can talk to your daughters this way but not your mother." I hung up.

My brothers and I were on the phone with each other often in the following days. One of them called the administrator at Mom's assisted living facility to ask if George had a history of preying on older women. (He was ten years younger than Mom, no spring chicken himself.) To their knowledge, no. Mom and George set up an appointment with my oldest brother to talk about financial arrangements. They set a date for their ceremony, a week and a half away. They would have married sooner, but Mom had to get a new pacemaker first. My mother, whose normal expectations pressed for family togetherness, casually dropped that they were exchanging vows in a park. We were welcome, but she assumed those of us who lived far away would not be able to attend.

My aunt Dot called three times before I picked up. I knew Mom had urged her to convince me that George was a good man. Dot had never met George. Aunt Dot was able to say, "I can see you kids are worried," which is more than Mom would admit. She also said, "Your mom sounds so happy."

Initially my oldest brother had the hardest time. He and his wife were the ones who'd be left to pick up the pieces if this all turned sour. They also feared having to take care of two aging people. I talked with my brother a few days later. He said he'd gotten over being mad, but he was grieving. He said, "I have to let her go. Like letting your daughter marry a jerk." He did meet with them over financial matters. He refused to take Mom shopping for a wedding dress, so George took her to Walmart, where she purchased a short navy-blue dress with a triangular lace inset at the neck. In the process, she lost one hearing aid, which my brother had to get replaced. She either mislaid her billfold or someone walked off with it when they were purchasing wedding rings, so my brother spent a full afternoon closing one account and opening another. When he visited her, she had him searching for lost earrings, one pearl and one black. She had only one of each in her jewelry box and insisted the staff must have stolen them. Only later did she realize she was wearing one pearl and one black earring. My brother hadn't noticed.

My other brother, who lives in Missouri, announced that he would not attend the wedding. With such late notice, tickets were expensive. He said, "She's made up her mind. I'm not going to stress over it." I decided to go and flew out the night before the wedding.

It's a surreal experience to stand in your ninety-six-year-old mother's assisted living apartment and help her dress for her wedding. I had purchased a pair of earrings for Mom, something "new." She was giddy, giggling and primping. She looked beautiful, her face relaxed and smiling, curly white hair framing her face.

I had planned my visit so I could be there after the ceremony, assuming that we would all go to lunch together. A family reception, of sorts.

"Oh, no," Mom said. "We're leaving right afterward to go on our honeymoon. That's what people do, isn't it?"

We drove to an expansive park in Fort Collins. The August day shone bright and cool. Mom was chilly so she wore an old striped blue and cream cardigan over her new dress. I met George, who was dressed in a brown suit, shirt and tie, gregarious, big smile. George's son, his wife, and one grandson were there. My brother's daughter was able to get off work. She informed her grandmother that more of the family would have come if they'd had more notice. Mom shrugged and grinned. An old friend of George's officiated at the short ceremony. A large bouquet of red roses sat atop a stone wall. Mom held the roses in a makeshift bouquet for a wedding picture. When the traditional minister asked, "Who gives this woman in marriage," my brother stepped forward, as requested, and sheepishly said, "I do."

At one point, George's daughter-in-law leaned over and whispered from the side of her mouth. "Did you know about this?"

"Not really," I said. "Did you?"

She widened her eyes and shook her head.

When the brief ceremony ended, Mom and George greeted everyone. Then they walked off, hand in hand. They planned to spend a couple nights honeymooning before returning to Fort Collins, when Mom would move into George's townhome.

That September, both of my brothers, their spouses, my husband, and I took an Alaskan cruise together. The first evening we gathered in my brother's stateroom to share a bottle of wine and—what else—talk about Mom. I told my brother from Missouri that the wedding was sweet. I said, "What choice did she have? Either embrace this chance at life or die alone in that assisted living place."

"If you felt that way, why were you so mad?" he asked.

A fair question. As was so often the case with Mom, it wasn't the thing itself but the way it was handled. She discounted the three of us, after years of commanding our devotion. My oldest brother had said, "She's throwing us out of her life." I wrote his comment in my journal and added, "I don't see that, but she is saying get the hell out of this; it has nothing to do with you." We made various predictions as to the success or failure of this new union. None of our fears were realized. George and Mom had a lovely year and a half together. My brother and sister-in-law who live in Fort Collins embraced George as part of the family and were won over by his dutiful attention to our mom. As my brother from Missouri predicted, Mom had George eating more vegetables and fruit. They played games endlessly. He drove her to visit the town she'd left behind. When she was diagnosed with lymphoma, he tended her for as long as he could. Eventually Mom had to be moved to a nursing home, but George visited her every day. She lived there only three months. I made frequent trips and sat by her bedside the day she died. She was ninety-eight years old.

I never warmed to George as much as my brother and his wife did. On the few occasions that I saw him, he talked mainly about himself. When I visited Fort Collins only a few months after Mom died, George had been invited to a family dinner. He showed up with a new wife. Though she was a likable person, I admit I bristled when I learned that George had proposed to her before he proposed to Mom. She had turned him down. Clearly, this was a man who could not be alone.

But then, what did any of that matter? He made my mother happy in the last grand episode of her life. She defied all of us and all odds, took a chance on love, and stepped off a cliff. To discover that life can be surprising and full of beauty at age ninety-six is a legacy to leave behind.

I miss my mom. I miss her as I knew her through all the stages of my life: the busy working mother who still found time to decorate for holidays, the champion pie-baker, the relentless game player, the limber great-grandmother who sat on the floor to play blocks with a toddler, her delight in little children, her off-key singing. But what I cling to and aspire to is her amazing resilience, her ability to adapt to changing circumstances and embrace the next good thing, her belief that there will always be a next good thing.

Last weekend, for my birthday, my husband and I took a trip down the Mississippi River and stopped in Wabasha at a gift shop called the Local World Gallery. The proprietor, Rob, was there, and we enjoyed a reunion of old friendship. Rob had played in the band of an original rock opera I had directed twelve years ago. The script was written by a friend and performed in our church. Rob's comment was, "Had any of us known how much work that was going to be, I'm not sure we would have taken it on."

After a while, Rob told me that I had inspired a song he'd written and recorded on one of his recent CDs. He picked up a guitar and sang a few verses of a song titled "Flying Leap," about starting over and trusting faith to lead you to the next adventure. I was touched and flattered but puzzled. "Are you sure that's me?" I asked.

He recited a few things he knew about me. Then he said, "You're the queen of flying leaps."

Oh, Rob. You should have met my mother.

What Is the Meaning of This?

Once, I ran over somebody's cat. If I hadn't been on my way to lunch, it wouldn't have happened. If I had stayed in my home office, writing the class proposal due on Monday, the cat would still be alive. If I hadn't forgotten where the restaurant was located and pulled over to the curb to consult a Minneapolis city map, the cat would have crossed safely behind me. Everything came down to timing and unbearable coincidence. Surely you can see that. If the cat had been distracted by a spring warbler or caught its tail in a slamming screen door—there are a million different things that could have happened—the cat would not be lying dead in the street.

To add to my guilt, I was driving an SUV, a Jeep Cherokee to be exact, a gas-guzzling symbol of privilege, a car that not only raised me above large portions of the world's population but sat so high that nosing up over a small rise on 54th Street, I did not see the black and white cat until it was too late. The cat streaked from my left, racing against gravity and the laws of physics, and as my foot touched the brake, I knew it was too late. I felt the sickening bump. If I had not tried to stop, the cat may have miraculously dodged between the wheels of my killer car.

I heard someone gasp and shout, Oh my god. Since I was alone, I knew it must be my voice, my breath rasping, but I was busy shepherding my car to the curb. As I repeated under my breath, I'm sorry, I'm sorry, I'm sorry, my mind played back scenes of my brothers standing night after night with the porch door open, calling into the black void for the return of Laddie, our beloved collie who had disappeared, run over, we suspected, by the reckless teenaged son of our neighbors up the road. The memory of my stricken brothers vacillated with images of my daughter cradling her two cats, Peanut and Rose.

Not only because of the cat's demise, but partly because of that, I have lately been contemplating the meaning of things. I was introduced to the concept of meaning, in a flat-footed, literal way, by Mrs. Eastman, the librarian in my Nebraska hometown. I discovered the library when I was ten years old. We had moved to town from the country, and for the first time, I could get my hands on all the books I wanted. I quickly filled up a card and then another and another. Mrs. Eastman seemed ancient to me, white hair coiled in a bun with hairpins that stuck out like miniature croquet hoops. Hose seams crawled up the backs of her legs, and she wore black, lace-up oxfords, old-lady shoes. When she leaned close, I could smell caked face powder and Evening in Paris cologne. The skin on her neck hung in droopy sacks. Her mid-calf length dresses were gray or navy blue, pinned at the neck with a cameo brooch. Sometimes, she wrapped her shoulders in a mouse-gray shawl. Rimless glasses slid down the length of her nose, and her back was humped.

The kids with whom I was trying to make friends, town kids whom I believed to be sophisticated and clever, did not like Mrs. Eastman, because she was crabby about noise and old and scary. If I was in the library with my friends, I ignored her, as they did. But if I came to the library alone, which happened more often, she was kind to me. I knew she liked me. I was the sort of kid teachers and old people favored, quiet and well behaved. And, I realize now, no librarian could resist such an avid reader.

By the time I was between my seventh- and eighth-grade years, the library had become a hangout for the prepubescent set. With no obvious plan, we'd show up at the library in the evening, whisper in the aisles, release dangerous pheromones into the air, plant secret notes in the "A" encyclopedia. Screened from Mrs. Eastman's desk by a tall bookcase, we sat at a wooden table with six chairs. We could read or talk or kick ankles under the table secure from the gaze of Mrs. Eastman. Better yet, if she decided to check on us, disturbed by the flirting and giggling, we could hear the clomp of her shoes rounding the turn by the giant dictionary on a stand. Her feet acted as our sentry, clattering across bare oak boards.

One summer evening I showed up at the library expecting to see my chief love interest, a laughing boy who once memorized the a-to-abasia page of the dictionary to impress me. Instead, when I walked in, the library was quiet as a stone. Mrs. Eastman stood at her desk, arms propped, trembling with rage. "You—" She pointed a finger at me. "Come with me."

I followed her around the bend, past the globe and the encyclo-pedias, breathing in book dust and leather. "There!" She pointed her finger at the varnished wooden table. In ballpoint ink, heavily traced but not quite carved into the wood, was my name with a heart around it and an arrow piercing it. "What is the meaning of this?" she said.

Dumbstruck, I could not answer. The meaning? What, exactly, did she want to know?

I thought of Mrs. Eastman as I moved from house to house on the street adjacent to the scene where I had killed a stranger's cat. I knocked on door after door. At one house the front door was unlocked, and I moved up onto a glassed-in porch. Lined up by the door were three pairs of shoes, the smallest a pair of toddler's white slip-on tennies. Oh, please, I whimpered, not here. Don't let it be here.

Next door to the house with the toddler shoes, an elderly woman warily cracked open her door. She was the only person I found home, at midday, in rows of houses on city streets. She held the door ajar, and I blurted out my confession like a penitent sinner. "I ran over somebody's cat," I wailed. "Was it yours?"

To her credit, she did not slam the door in my face. She stood her ground and, with considerable kindness, said, "Oh no, dear. I don't have a cat."

"It was black and white." My voice threatened to escalate into hysteria. "It didn't have tags. I hope it didn't belong to those little kids next door."

"No, no," she said. She had peach-colored hair and wore a purple paisley dress and three rings on her left hand. More stylish, but about the same age as Mrs. Eastman. "They don't have a cat."

I put my hand over my heart, felt my own chest heaving with the exertion of maintaining a thin edge of control. "Do you know whose it is?" I asked.

"Try the house behind mine, across the alley. They have a cat they let run loose."

"Thank you," I said. She closed the door.

I turned the woman's phrase over in my mind as I continued my search for the owner of the cat I had killed. They have a cat they let run loose. An implied judgment. Perhaps I could let myself off the hook and blame the owner's negligence. Maybe, even, I should sue them for causing me emotional hardship. All the while, I knew this trick wouldn't work, because my daughter let her two cats run loose.

The house across the alley had a walk littered with toys. Shrubbery hugged the porch and hadn't been trimmed for years. An empty leash hung from the screen door latch, and when I stepped up to ring the bell, a dog barked ferociously behind the door. I waited on the step for what seemed a long time, the dog growing more and more agitated, and finally I walked away. I had not found the owners of the cat. No one would lovingly carry it home. No one would bury it in the backyard with tender rituals of remembrance. There would be no closure for whoever might be longing for the cat's return. Defeated, I got into my car and, barely glancing back, I drove away.

Writers are in the business of searching for meaning. We are on the lookout for oddities, moments of revelation, quirks in human behavior, unexpected connections, intriguing bits and pieces that we work like beads on an abacus. We worry about stealing moments from lives of those we love. Can I possibly reveal Uncle Albert's alcoholism? Even if fictionalized, won't my mother know I'm writing about that time she hiked across a corral carrying two suitcases? Yet, what greater gift could we offer than to suggest that someone's life is a worthy subject for a story or an essay or a poem? If we could learn to step back, examine our own lives and the ordinary moments in them with rigor and compassion, wouldn't we also learn to peel back the daily inertia, the boring overlay of gauzy inattention, and lay bare the gems of meaning?

Once, I ran over a cat. I have lived to tell of the experience. I've written about it, raised it to the level of worthy subject. And still, I would rather it hadn't happened.

Once I knew a boy who liked me but was too shy to tell me, so he defaced public property to leave me a message.

Mrs. Eastman produced a bucket and a sponge, directed me to a bathroom in the basement, then stood over me while I scrubbed at the top of the table, wiping away my name and many others. I knew that she was disappointed in me, and while I was innocent of this petty crime of carving, I was guilty of betraying her by conspiring with my noisy friends. She eventually left me and went back to her desk, and I labored, hotly, my arm aching, all the time wondering: What is the meaning of this? What *is* the meaning of this?

Acknowledgments

Since one theme of these stories is that memories are fluid and change over time, I hope I will be forgiven if my renditions don't match the facts as you, the reader, might remember them. I realize, for instance, that my description of Mrs. Eastman is a composite of many older women I knew as a child. I can assure you, however, that the emotional impact of that encounter has stayed with me. I do want to thank the real librarian Mrs. Eastman represents and all other librarians who were kind to me and set me on a path to lifelong reading.

By the way, Mrs. Eastman is not her real name. I have changed many names throughout these essays. I decided to do this after one of my brilliant team of physicians during my cancer treatment said I could write anything I wanted about her or any others, as long as I changed the names. I hope this will be understood as an act of courtesy and not an artful dodge.

I have had the good fortune to have influential mentors in my life. Don Keyworth, a philosophy professor for many years at Drake University, stretched my thinking. Though my husband and I met Don and his wife, Colleen, after we had graduated from college, we were both students of Don's probing mind. The Keyworths spent summers on Pelican Lake in Minnesota in a 1930s cottage that had been owned by Don's mother. On the cabin-length porch stood an oversized king bed that served as a couch during the day. Brad and I took turns sitting on the bed, atop a red striped chenille spread, while Don sat in his desk chair alongside, and together we did philosophy. Colleen added the spice and creativity to our long relationship. The four of us loved to play charades and once challenged ourselves by acting out whole Bible verses selected by opening the book and randomly setting a finger down. My favorite was from the book of Ecclesiastes:

"Dead flies can make a whole bottle of perfume stink" ("as a little folly outweighs wisdom," but we left that part out).

Sally Hill, one of the first Presbyterian women to be ordained, ushered me into the world of ecumenical activities by inviting me to sit on various committees with the Minneapolis Council of Churches and to participate in the 1993 Re-Imagining Conference that was held in Minneapolis. We shared a love of fiber arts, reveled in a good book, became exasperated over politics, and always, always laughed a lot.

One of the things that happens with age is that losses accumulate. I miss Don, Colleen, and Sally, as I miss so many others. I am grateful for these friends, who believed in me and encouraged me. In their memory, I hope I can do the same for others.

I am grateful for my friends from Judson Baptist Church in Minneapolis, my neighborhood, my writing pals from Hamline's MFA program, long-time friends who may be distant in miles but never in my heart, and friends I've gathered along the way when my life luckily intersected with theirs. You make my daily life rich and nourishing.

A special nod to Susan Malouf, my theater partner at Role Over Productions, who was the first person to suggest that my work could go beyond my study walls. Many thanks to Mary Bednarowski, who finds time to read my rough drafts. Thanks to my readers who make this endeavor seem worthwhile.

I have had the privilege of working with the University of Nebraska Press several times. Their professionalism, respect for writers, and dedication to making beautiful books has made my task easier. This time around, a special thanks to Clark Whitehorn, who chose the book, and to my copyeditor Stephanie Marshall Ward, and to all the staff, including Abbey Frankforter, Tish Fobben, Sarah Kee, and Lindsey Welch. Everyone with whom I've had contact has been a pleasure to work with.

Last, but never least, thank you to my wonderful family, Joerns and Carters: brothers, sisters-in-law, brothers-in law, nieces and nephews and their spouses and their children. Thank you to our daughters, Shannon and Raegan, our son-in-law, Jacob, and our four grandchildren, Nadine, Elijah, Henry, and Tyson, who are the delight and center of our love and devotion. To Brad, my partner for over fifty years, how could we have known when our first date nearly blew up that we would share this lifelong love affair, grow together, and grow old together.

Versions of two of these essays were previously published: "Memory Theft and Transplants" first appeared in *Water~Stone*, Fall, 2001; "What Is the Meaning of This?" in *Intro Quarterly*, vol. 3.

Notes

Looking for Direction

1. My eldest brother remembers this differently. He says our small house was better than most migrant workers' houses. He's right about that, but still, I remember hearing my mother refer to it as "the beet shack." My brother says we called it Degraw, as it was near Degraw school.
2. My grandfather's neck was broken when he was knocked backward off a haystack. He was moved to the university hospital in Omaha. My mother told stories of him being placed in the basement where his cries of pain would not disturb other patients. My dad's sister, Addie, had lost two husbands in farm accidents, borne four children, taken on four stepchildren, and lost her oldest son in a drowning accident, all by the time she was thirty-two.

Salvador Dalí and Me

1. Dalí's original painting, *The Persistence of Memory*, is in the permanent collection of the Museum of Modern Art in New York City. The painting is small, about the size of a laptop, but it is still considered one of the premier examples of surrealistic art.

In Pursuit of Magic

1. This is what Samuel Taylor Coleridge called the "willing suspension of disbelief" in his treatise on poetic faith, 1817.

My Mother, the Liar

1. Eventually my mother had three husbands, but at the time of this conversation, she'd been married only twice.

Carnal Appetites

1. We always had chickens for eggs, and my mother enjoyed the thrill of seeing how many eggs she could get to hatch under a setting hen. Raising chickens for sale began as a business venture for my two older brothers.

My parents kept track of the cost of the baby chickens and the feed and subtracted that from the profits when the chickens were sold. One year my brothers used the proceeds to purchase a waffle iron for my parents' Christmas gift. We had a large chest freezer and kept the unsold chickens for ourselves.

Privilege

1. I was admitted to the MFA program at Hamline University. I loved being immersed in a community of writers. I had wonderful teachers, especially Barrie Jean Borich, Sheila O'Connor, and Mary Rockcastle. I cherish my writing buddies, many of whom have become published authors and poets.

I Say Unicorns Are Real

1. This is a cousin to Coleridge's "willing suspension of disbelief." Only here, I am thinking of Shakespeare, "There are more things in Heaven and Earth, Horatio, than are dreamt of in your philosophy."